My World

ADVENTURES IN TIME AND PLACE

D0103076

James A. Banks

Barry K. Beyer

Gloria Contreras

Jean Craven

Gloria Ladson-Billings

Mary A. McFarland

Walter C. Parker

NATIONAL GEOGRAPHIC SOCIETY

THIS DOLL WAS MADE IN THE 1920S. MANY THINGS TODAY ARE DIFFERENT FROM HOW THEY WERE LONG AGO. BUT CHILDREN STILL HAVE TOYS THAT ARE SPECIAL TO THEM.

THE PRINCETON REVIEW

McGraw-Hill

New York   Farmington

PROGRAM AUTHORS

Dr. James A. Banks
Professor of Education and
  Director of the Center for
  Multicultural Education
University of Washington
Seattle, Washington

Dr. Barry K. Beyer
Professor Emeritus, Graduate
  School of Education
George Mason University
Fairfax, Virginia

Dr. Gloria Contreras
Professor of Education
University of North Texas
Denton, Texas

Jean Craven
District Coordinator of
  Curriculum Development
Albuquerque Public Schools
Albuquerque, New Mexico

Dr. Gloria Ladson-Billings
Professor of Education
University of Wisconsin
Madison, Wisconsin

Dr. Mary A. McFarland
Instructional Coordinator of
  Social Studies, K–12, and
  Director of Staff Development
Parkway School District
Chesterfield, Missouri

Dr. Walter C. Parker
Professor and Program Chair for
  Social Studies Education
University of Washington
Seattle, Washington

NATIONAL GEOGRAPHIC SOCIETY
Washington, D.C.

CONSULTANTS FOR TEST PREPARATION

THE PRINCETON REVIEW

The Princeton Review is not affiliated
with Princeton University or ETS.

CALIFORNIA SENIOR CONSULTANT

Dr. Carlos E. Cortés
Professor Emeritus of History
University of California
Riverside, California

CALIFORNIA PROGRAM CONSULTANTS

Diane Bowers
Former Assistant Director of Education
  for the Yurok Tribe
Klamath, California

Dr. Susan L. Douglass
Affiliated Scholar, Council on Islamic
  Education
Fountain Valley, California

Dr. Karen Nakai
Lecturer of History-Social Science
Department of Education
University of California
Irvine, California

Shelly Osborne
Teacher-Literacy Mentor
Franklin School
Alameda, California

Dr. Valerie Ooka Pang
Professor, School of Teacher Education
San Diego State University
San Diego, California

Lyn Reese
Director, Women in History Project
Berkeley, California

Dr. Curtis C. Roseman
Professor of Geography
University Of Southern California
Los Angeles, California

Dr. Robert M. Senkewicz
Professor of History
Santa Clara University
Santa Clara, California

Evelyn Staton
Librarian
San Francisco School District
Member, Multiethnic Literature Forum
  for San Francisco
San Francisco, California

Dr. Clifford E. Trafzer
Department of Ethnic Studies
University of California
Riverside, California

PROGRAM CONSULTANTS

Dr. John Bodnar
Professor of History
Indiana University
Bloomington, Indiana

Dr. Sheilah Clark-Ekong
Professor, Department of Anthropology
University of Missouri, St. Louis
St. Louis, Missouri

Dr. Darlene Clark Hine
John A. Hannah Professor of History
Michigan State University
East Lansing, Michigan

Dr. John L. Esposito
Professor of Religion and
  International Affairs
Georgetown University
Washington, D. C.

Dr. Gary Manson
Department of Geography
Michigan State University
East Lansing, Michigan

Dr. Juan Mora-Torrés
Professor of Latin American History
University of Texas at San Antonio
San Antonio, Texas

Dr. Joseph Rosenbloom
Professor, Classics Department
Washington University
St. Louis, Missouri

Dr. Robert Seltzer
Professor of Jewish History
Hunter College
City University of New York

Dr. Peter Stearns
Dean, College of Humanities
  and Social Studies
Carnegie Mellon University
Pittsburgh, Pennsylvania

CONSULTING AUTHORS

Dr. James Flood
Professor of Teacher Education, Reading
  and Language Development
San Diego State University
San Diego, California

Dr. Diane Lapp
Professor of Teacher Education, Reading
  and Language Development
San Diego State University
San Diego, California

GRADE-LEVEL CONSULTANTS

Patti Crandall
First Grade Teacher
Harbor Summit Elementary School
San Diego, California

Linda Baird Garner
First Grade Teacher
Dudley Elementary School
Fairport, New York

Joan Hinze
First Grade Teacher
Webster Elementary School
Watertown, Wisconsin

Marlene F. Kuskin
Elementary School Teacher
St. Joseph Collinwood Elementary School
Cleveland, Ohio

Gayle B. Morrison
First Grade Teacher
Woodrow Wilson Elementary School
Birmingham, Alabama

Josie Ramirez-Rey
First Grade Teacher
Chabot Elementary School
Oakland, California

Liz Rickett
First Grade Teacher
Washington Elementary School
Montebello, California

Kate Robertson
Assistant Principal
Sneed Elementary School
Houston, Texas

Pamela Shannon
Elementary School Teacher
Graystone School
San Jose, California

CONTRIBUTING WRITERS

Catherine M. Tamblyn
Little Silver, New Jersey

Linda Scher
Raleigh, North Carolina

Acknowledgments

The publisher gratefully acknowledges permission to reprint the following material:

Entire text and art, **Houses and Homes** by Ann Morris, photographs by Ken Heyman. Text Copyright © 1992 by Ann Morris.
"Exerpts", from **It's My Earth Too** by Kathleen Krull. Copyright © 1992. Used by permission of Dell Books, a division of Bantam
Doubleday Dell Publishing Group, Inc. **What Was It Like** by Charlotte Zolotow. Copyright © 1993 by Charlotte Zolotow. Published
by HarperCollins Children's. Used by permission of HarperCollins Children's. (continued on page R18)

McGraw-Hill School Division

A Division of The McGraw·Hill Companies

Copyright © 2000,1999 McGraw-Hill School Division,
a Division of the Educational and Professional
Publishing Group of The McGraw-Hill Companies, Inc.

All rights reserved. No part of this book may be reproduced or
transmitted in any form or by any means, electronic or mechanical,
including photocopying, recording, or by any information storage and
retrieval system, without permission in writing from the publisher.

McGraw-Hill School Division
Two Penn Plaza
New York, New York 10121

Printed in the United States of America

ISBN 002148821-5

1 2 3 4 5 6 7 8 9 004 03 02 01 00 99

CONTENTS

UNIT ONE
2

Where We Live

UNIT TWO
42

We Belong

UNIT THREE
72

People at Work

UNIT FOUR
102

Our World

UNIT FIVE
142

It Happened in America

UNIT SIX
182

Americans Celebrate

REFERENCE SECTION

STANDARDIZED TEST SUPPORT

THE PRINCETON REVIEW

FEATURES

SKILLS

CITIZENSHIP

MANY VOICES

CHARTS & GRAPHS

MAPS

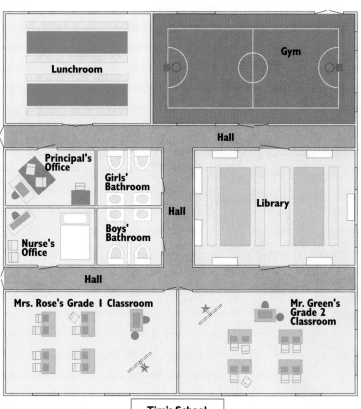

Lunchroom

Gym

Hall

Principal's Office

Girls' Bathroom

Nurse's Office

Boys' Bathroom

Hall

Library

Hall

Mrs. Rose's Grade 1 Classroom

Mr. Green's Grade 2 Classroom

Tim's School

YOUR TEXTBOOK
at a glance

Your book is called *My World: Adventures in Time and Place*. It has many parts.

NATIONAL GEOGRAPHIC

Look at Your World

What does this place have that other places don't have?

What makes the beach a fun place to be?

One special part of your book is called Look at Your World. It shows places in our country.

Your book has six units. Each unit has many lessons. You will learn new things in each lesson.

LESSON 1

Here We Are

School

Welcome Class!

This is Tim's first day at school. His school is in Austin, Texas. "Welcome," says Mrs. Rose. Mrs. Rose is Tim's teacher.

4

Some units Close with a Story. Others close with a poem or a song.

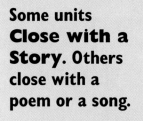

The world is full of houses . . .

CITIZENSHIP
Making Choices

A Playground Problem

Our class played outside today. Not everyone got along.

What rules does the class need to get along and play fairly?*

We should put these things away.

Why should we? We didn't use them last.

CITIZENSHIP
Making a Difference

CALIFORNIA
Los Angeles

Ralph Sanders is the teacher who started the club. He takes the cans to a place where they can be reused. The club gets paid for each can. They use the money to buy trees for the schoolyard. These trees make the neighborhood a nicer place.

Yvette says, "I feel happy because we are making the earth feel better."

Tim sat next to Ann. She drew a picture of her house. Her house is red. Tim drew a picture of his house. His house is white.

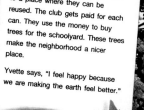

Some special lessons tell about people who are Making a Difference. Others tell about **Making Choices.**

Look at the back of your book. The **Dictionary of Geographic Words** and **Picture Glossary** tell what words mean.

PICTURE GLOSSARY

Dictionary of GEOGRAPHIC WORDS

HILL Land that is higher than the land around it, but lower than a mountain.

PLAIN Flat land.

LAKE Body of water with land all around it.

NATIONAL GEOGRAPHIC

Look at Your World

What does this place have that other places don't have?

What makes the beach a fun place to be?

How do you get to school in the morning?

What do people do to help plants grow?

How does this boy know where he is?

UNIT ONE

Where We Live

Key Words

neighborhood

map

community

state

country

Earth

3

Here We Are

This is Tim's first day at school.
His school is in Los Angeles,
California. Mrs. Rose is Tim's
teacher.

Tim sat next to Ann. She drew a picture of her house. Her house is red. Tim drew a picture of his house. His house is white.

"What did you see on your way to school today?" asks Mrs. Rose.

Tim saw a library. Tim and Ann both saw a firehouse. Ann saw a church being built.

"You are both neighbors," says Mrs. Rose. "Neighbors are people who live near each other. You both live in the very same **neighborhood**. A neighborhood is a place where people live, work, and play."

1. What is a neighborhood?

2. What are some places in your neighborhood?

GEOGRAPHY SKILLS
Using Models and Maps

Here are some rooms in Tim's school. This is what the rooms would look like without a roof. Find the lunchroom.

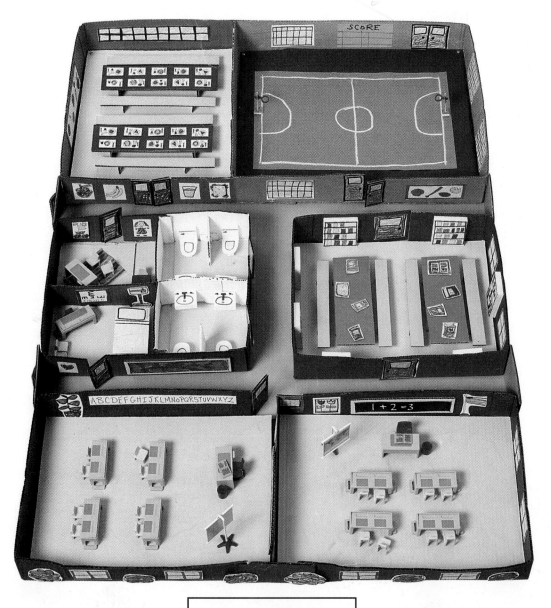

Tim's School

This is a **map** of the school. A map is a drawing of a place. Mrs. Rose's classroom is next to Mr. Green's classroom.

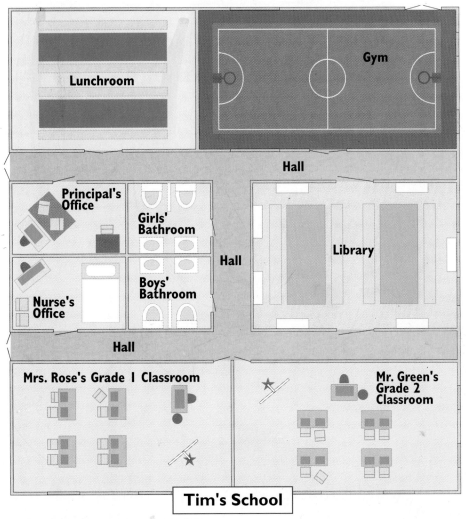

Lunchroom

Gym

Hall

Principal's Office

Girls' Bathroom

Nurse's Office

Boys' Bathroom

Hall

Library

Hall

Mrs. Rose's Grade 1 Classroom

Mr. Green's Grade 2 Classroom

Tim's School

Trying the Skill

Use the map to answer these questions.

1. Is the lunchroom near or far from the gym?

2. Is Mrs. Rose's classroom to the left or the right of Mr. Green's classroom?

3. How would a map of your classroom be helpful to you?

Our Homes Are in Neighborhoods

Mrs. Rose's class is putting up pictures.
They show different kinds of homes.

10

Neighborhoods are different too.
Some neighborhoods have many
homes and stores. Others have only a
few places.

This is Ann's house. Tim and his brother David ride by her house.

"Is this where you live?" Tim asks. "I did not know your address."

An address tells the number of a house. It also tells the name of a street.

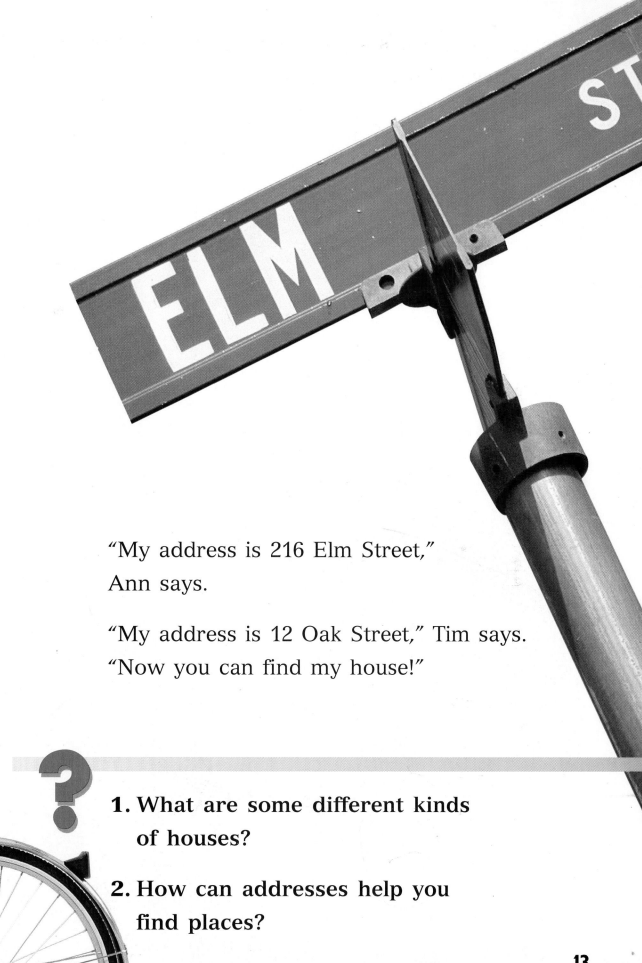

"My address is 216 Elm Street," Ann says.

"My address is 12 Oak Street," Tim says. "Now you can find my house!"

1. What are some different kinds of houses?

2. How can addresses help you find places?

Rochester

MICHIGAN

Caitlin and Compass

Meet Caitlin Littmann. Caitlin and her family joined the Puppy Program at Leader Dogs for the Blind.

The Puppy Program sent a puppy to Caitlin's family in Rochester, Michigan. Caitlin named the puppy Compass.

Someday Compass will help people who cannot see. She will help them to find their way.

It is Caitlin's job to help Compass get used to people. She takes the dog to places in her neighborhood.

One day Compass will live with a blind person. "I will be sad when Compass leaves our house," says Caitlin. But she will also be very proud of Compass.

Neighborhoods Are in Communities

We all live in neighborhoods. We also live in bigger places called **communities**. A community has many neighborhoods.

Meg lives near a town called Bend, Oregon. A town is a small community.

Meg lives on a ranch. A ranch is a big farm. Meg's family raises horses and cattle.

Ranches are far apart from each other. Meg cannot see her neighbor's house.

Paul lives far away from
Meg. He lives in a city.
A city is a big community.
Paul lives in the city of
Atlanta, Georgia.

Many people live and work in Atlanta. There are many places to see and things to do.

1. What is a community?

2. Is your community more like Meg's or Paul's? Tell why.

Looking from Above

Paul and his father took a trip on a
plane. They looked down at a
community. This is what they saw.

This is a map of the same community.
What do you see?

1. How is the map like the picture?
   How is it different?

2. What would you see if you looked at
   your community from a plane?

GEOGRAPHY SKILLS
Using Map Keys

Many maps use symbols. Symbols are drawings that stand for something else. What do these symbols stand for? a tree; a house

 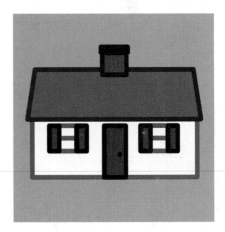

Maps with symbols have a map key. The map key tells what each symbol means.

This is a map of Jim's community. Look at the map key. The swings are a symbol for a playground.

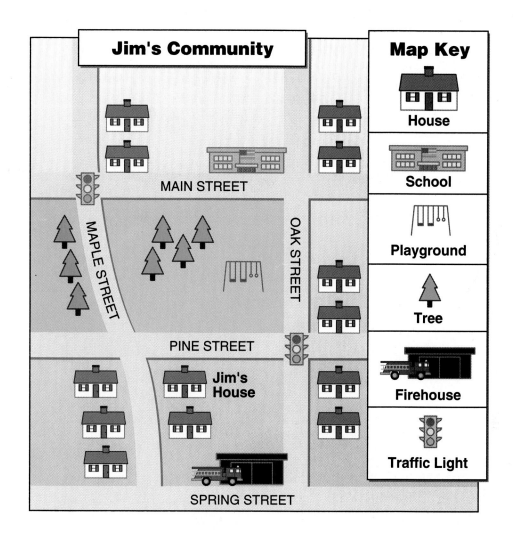

Trying the Skill

Use the map to answer these questions.

1. Name two buildings on this map.

2. On which street is Jim's school?

3. What symbols would you use to make a map of your community?

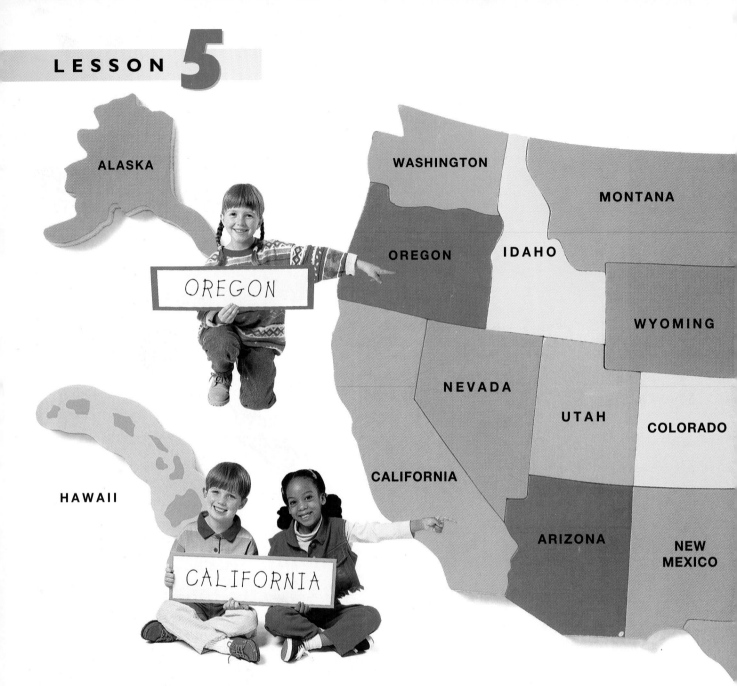

We Live in the United States

Communities are in a bigger place called a
state. This map shows 50 states. They
make up our country. A country is a land
and the people who live there. Our country
is the United States of America.

THE UNITED STATES
OF AMERICA

1. What is the name of our country?

2. How is a community like a state?
   How is it different?

Sharing Our Earth

You live in many places. You live in a home. Your home is part of a neighborhood. Your neighborhood is part of a community. Your community is part of a state. Your state is part of a country.

Countries are on Earth. Earth is our world. Earth is round. It is made up of land and water.

A globe is round like Earth. It shows how Earth looks. The blue parts show water. The green parts show land. Find the land on the globe.

Earth is a very big place. It is shared by all living things. What things in the pictures do you know about?

1. What is Earth?

2. Name three different places that you live in.

29

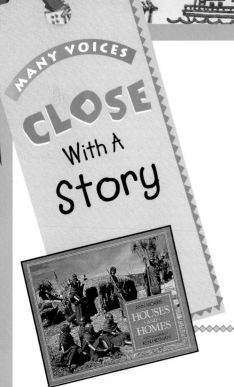

from

HOUSES
· AND ·
HOMES

by Ann Morris

Photographs by Ken Heyman

The world is full of houses . . .

big houses

little houses

bright houses

white houses

34

houses that move

and houses that stay

in a row

or all alone

filled with families

just right for one.

UNIT 1 REVIEW

Thinking About Words

Match the words to the pictures.

1. neighborhood **2.** community **3.** state
4. country **5.** Earth

a.
United States

b.

c.
California

d.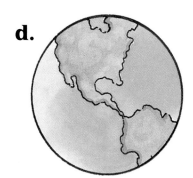

e.

Thinking About Ideas

1. What are neighbors?
2. What does an address tell?
3. Name two kinds of communities.
4. Tell how you can live in a state and a country at the same time.

Tell about a place that you like in your community. Tell why you like it.

Using Skills

Reviewing Using Maps

1. Look at the map below. What does it show?
2. Is the flag near or far from the door?
3. Who sits behind Bob?

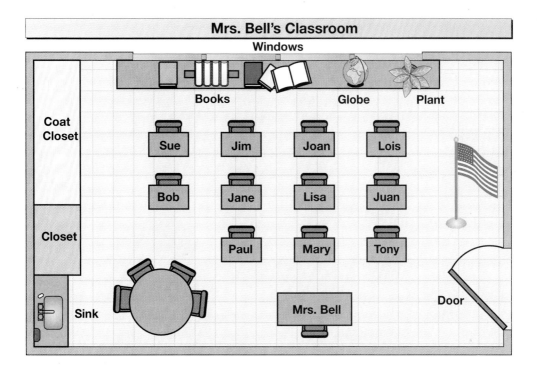

Mrs. Bell's Classroom

Make Your Own!

- Draw a map of the place where you play.
- Add the things you play with.

Using Skills

Reviewing Using Map Keys

1. What does the map show?
2. What symbol stands for the library?
3. How many stores are on the map?

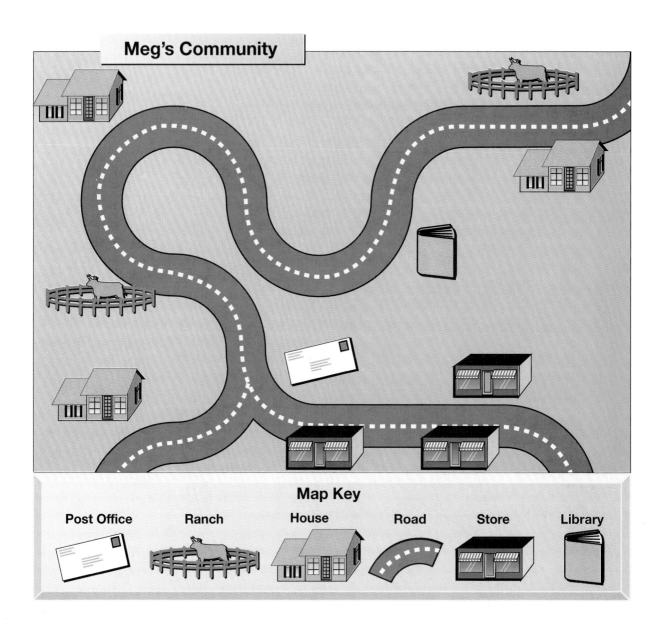

Meg's Community

Map Key

| Post Office | Ranch | House | Road | Store | Library |

UNIT REVIEW PROJECT

Make a "Here I Am" Book

- Draw a picture of yourself. Write your name under the picture.
- Draw your school. Write the name of your school.
- Draw some places in your neighborhood.
- Make a cover for your book.
- Staple the pages together.

Reading on Your Own

You can look for these books at your library.

UNIT TWO
We Belong

Key Words

family

group

rule

law

vote

citizen

President

Family and Friends

My name is Roberto Ramos. Here is my **family**. People in a family help and care for each other. They play together too.

My grandparents, aunt and uncle, and cousins also belong to my family. Sometimes they visit on special days like birthdays.

Not all families are like mine. Some are bigger. Others are smaller. Sometimes a whole family does not live together.

My family

Roberto

Each family is special. Here are some pictures of my friends and their families.

?

1. Tell one way that families are the same.

2. Name some people in your family.

People Together

Roberto belongs to many **groups**. People who do things together make up a group.

You and your family are one group. Your class is a group. Your friends are also a group.

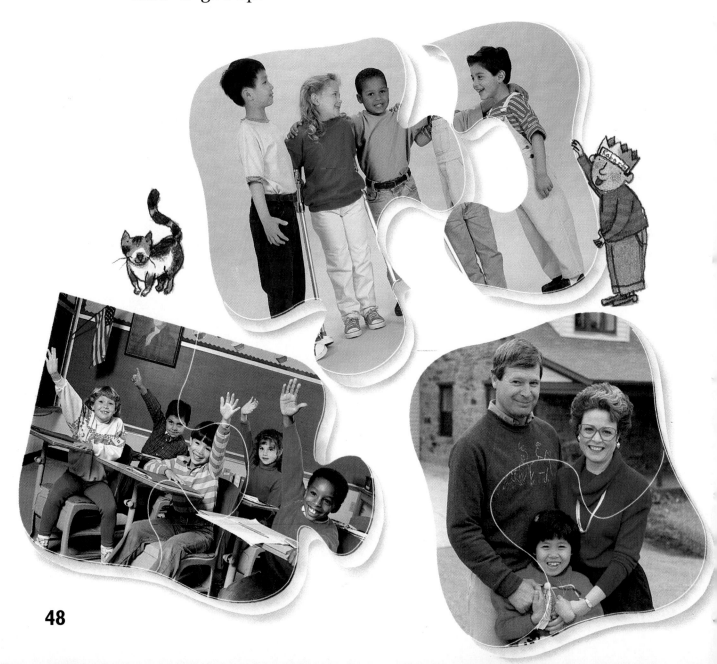

People in groups work and play together.
They need to get along with each other.
They work together to make choices.

1. Why do people work in groups?

2. What groups are you part of?

THINKING SKILLS
Finding Alike and Different

Things that are the same are alike. The pictures below are alike. Each shows a group of people. In what other ways are they alike?

Things that are not alike are different. These pictures are different because they show different families. In what other ways are they different?

Trying the Skill

Use the pictures on this page to answer the questions.

1. Name two ways the pictures are alike.

2. Name two ways they are different.

3. How can you tell if things are alike or different?

Getting Along

Police Officer Smith is visiting Roberto's school. "We get along if we follow **rules**," says Officer Smith. "Some rules tell us what to do. Some rules tell us what not to do."

How
We Follow
Rules

Rules help us get along in school. They help to keep us safe too.

Look at the pictures. Who is following the rules? Tell how these rules help us.

School Rules

A **law** is a rule that all people must follow. "These pictures show rules and laws," says Officer Smith. "Following them will help keep you safe."

54

Officer Smith takes the children for a walk. "Some laws are on signs," he says. "Signs tell you what you must do. They tell you what you must not do."

1. How do rules and laws help you get along with others? How do they keep you safe?

2. What new rule does your class need?

CITIZENSHIP
Making Choices

A Playground Problem

Our class played outside today. Not everyone got along.

What rules does the class need to get along and play fairly?

They won't let me use the swings.

No! I was first.

I was first.

57

STUDY SKILLS
Using Charts

Charts show things using words and pictures. The title tells you what the chart is about.

Read across the chart. "Raise hands" is a rule for school. Which rules are for home?

Rules for Home, School, and Play				
	Raise hands	Share with others	Don't push	Hang up your clothes
School	✔	✔	✔	✔
Home		✔	✔	✔
Play		✔	✔	

Trying the Skill

This chart shows how Roberto's class will help the teacher. Use it to answer the questions below.

Ways to Help in Class				
	Put away books	Clean chalkboard	Feed class rabbit	Pass paper and crayons
Roberto	✔			
Sara		✔		
Mike				✔
Joan			✔	

1. How many children will help?

2. How will Sara help?

3. Who will feed Peter, the class rabbit?

4. How can charts be helpful?

Your Vote Counts

People may want different things. They can **vote** for what they want. To vote means to choose something.

Roberto's family is voting. What will they do after dinner? Everyone wants to do a puzzle except Roberto's sister.

Roberto's class voted on what to do after lunch. Voting is a fair way to make choices.

Look at the chart. What did most children want to do?

Our Class Activity
1. Sing   X X X X
2. Play a game XXXXXXX
3. Listen to a story X X X X X
4. Paint X X X X

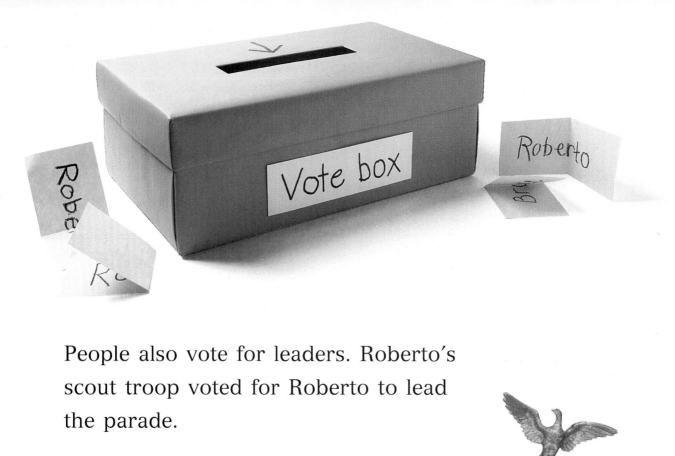

People also vote for leaders. Roberto's scout troop voted for Roberto to lead the parade.

United States citizens vote for leaders. A citizen is a person who belongs to a country. People who are born in the United States are citizens of our country. People from other countries can become citizens too.

Citizens who are 18 years old can vote. They can vote for the President of the United States. The President is the head of our country.

1. Why do people vote?

2. What kinds of things do you vote about at school and at home?

Family and Friends in Japan

こんにわは

UNITED STATES

JAPAN

Konnichiwa! That means "hello." My name is Miko Ota. I live in Japan.

This is my family. We love and care for one another. My grandfather and grandmother live with us.

I walk to school with my friends. We follow rules to keep us safe. We wear yellow hats to school. Drivers see us when we cross streets.

Children in Japan work very hard in school. I like reading and writing.

Sayonara! Goodbye!

さようなら

?

1. Miko is part of which groups?

2. How is Miko's life like yours? How is it different?

CLOSE With A Song

MANY VOICES

The World

Words and Music by Ella Jenkins

Oh the world is big ___ and the world is small ___ so there's

lots of room ___ for the short and the tall. Oh the

world is far ___ and the world is wide ___ but there are

The World Is Big, The World Is Small

man - y dif-fer-ent ways to see the oth - er side. 1.You can
2.You can

tra - vel in a boat, you can tra - vel in a plane, you can
tra - vel on a bus, you can tra - vel in a train, you can

tra - vel in a dance, you can tra - vel in a game.
tra - vel in a song, you can tra - vel in a name.

UNIT 2 REVIEW

Thinking About Words

Use these words to finish the sentences.

family	group	rules	law
vote	citizens	President	

1. A _____ is a rule that all people must follow.

2. People in a _____ love and care for each other.

3. People who do things together are a _____.

4. People get along when they follow _____.

5. To _____ means to choose something.

6. The _____ is the head of our country.

7. People who live in a country are called _____.

Thinking About Ideas

1. What are some things families do together?

2. Why do people belong to groups?

3. How do laws help people?

4. What happens if people don't follow rules?

5. Why is voting a good way to choose something?

SHARE WITH A FRIEND

What groups are you a part of?

How are the groups alike and different?

Using Skills

Reviewing Using Charts

1. What does the chart show?
2. How does Roberto help at home?
3. Which job do Alma and her dad share?
4. What job does Roberto's mom do?

Ramos Family	Wash and Dry Dishes	Dust	Feed Cat	Set Table	Take Out Garbage
JOBS WE DO AT HOME					
Roberto			✓	✓	
Alma	✓	✓			
Mom					✓
Dad	✓				

Make Your Own!

- Make a job chart for a group to which you belong. Write a name for your chart.
- Write some of the group's jobs at the top.
- Write the names of the people on the side.
- Mark the boxes to show their jobs.

Helping At the Park

Friends	Plant	Water	Paint	Clean up
Cindy	✓			✓
Ian			✓	✓
Sam		✓	✓	✓
Patti	✓			✓

Using Skills

Reviewing Finding Alike and Different

Use the pictures to answer the questions.

1. In what ways are the pictures alike?
2. In what ways is the girl different in these pictures?
3. In what ways is the family different in these pictures?
4. In what ways are you alike or different from the girl in these pictures?

Gail's Family

Gail's Family

70

UNIT REVIEW PROJECT

Make a Puzzle

- Draw a picture of a group to which you belong.
- Cut your picture into puzzle pieces.
- Have a friend put your puzzle together.

Reading on Your Own

You can look for these books at your library.

UNIT THREE

People at Work

Key Words

job	needs
goods	shelter
service	wants
volunteer	transportation

We Have Jobs

My name is Pam. It is my **job** to feed my dog. A job is work that people do.

My mom, dad, and sister Lisa have jobs at home too. We like to work together.

Mom and Dad also have jobs away from home. They get money for their work.

Mom works in a bakery. Her job is to bake good things to eat.

My dad works in a hospital. His job is to take pictures of bones.

Some people make or grow things.
Things people make or grow are called
goods. My mom makes bread.

Some people do things for other people.
This work is called a **service**. My dad
helps people get well.

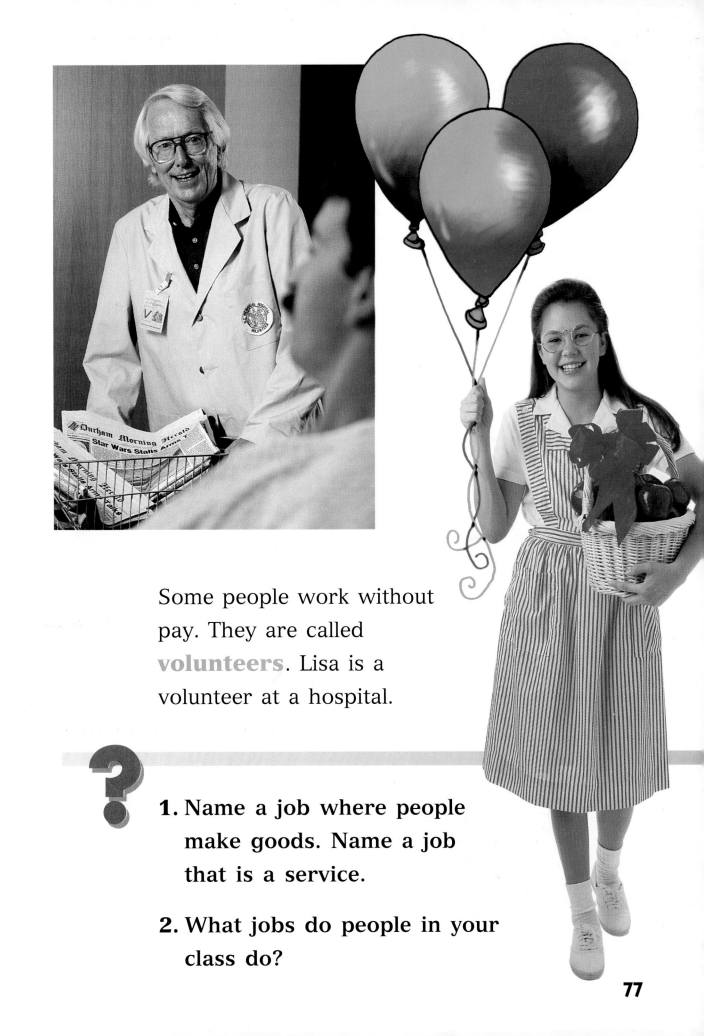

Some people work without pay. They are called **volunteers**. Lisa is a volunteer at a hospital.

?

1. Name a job where people make goods. Name a job that is a service.

2. What jobs do people in your class do?

Our Needs and Wants

All people have **needs**. Needs are things we must have to live. Everyone needs water and food. Apples are my favorite food.

Everyone needs **shelter** too. A shelter is a place to live.

People need clothes. Some clothes help us to stay cool. Other clothes keep us warm and dry.

People also need love and care. How do people love and care for others?

People have **wants** too. Wants are things we would like to have. I want dancing lessons. My sister wants a computer. My mom and dad want to take a family trip.

We cannot have all that we want. My family buys the things we need. Then we sometimes get the things we want.

Sometimes people cannot buy things they need. My family helps other people at a special shelter. At the shelter people get food, clothing, and a place to stay.

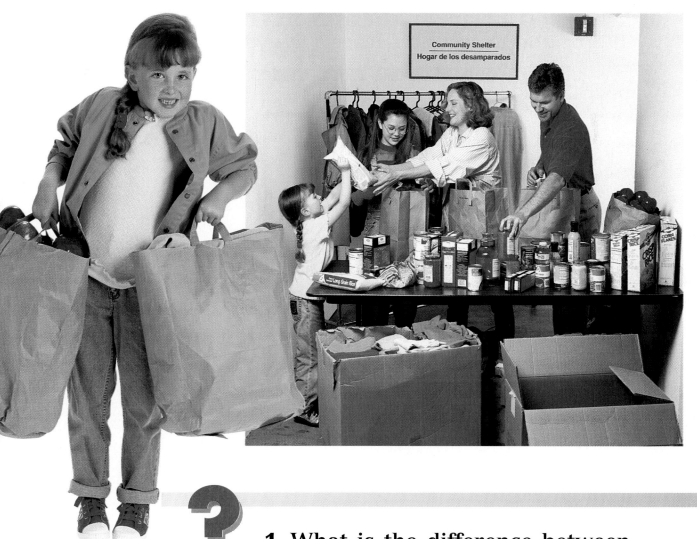

1. What is the difference between needs and wants?

2. Why do people have to choose what they buy?

CITIZENSHIP
Making Choices

How Should We Spend Our Money?

Pam's class sold cookies at the school fair. They made $50.00. The class does not agree on how to spend the money. Everyone has a different idea. Help the class to decide.

A tree for our school

Moving Goods and People

We can buy things we need and want at stores. These pictures show how pants get to a store.

84

Trains are one kind of **transportation**. Transportation moves people or things from one place to another. How do the pants get from the train to the store?

Transportation takes goods to and from the United States and other countries. Look at the pictures. What kinds of transportation do you see?

What kinds of transportation does your community have?

1. What is transportation?

2. How does transportation help people?

THINKING SKILLS
Sorting Things into Groups

Pam wanted to sort these pictures into groups. To sort things, she put together things that are alike.

Pam looked at one picture. She looked for others like it. She sorted the pictures of the school bus, plane, and boat into one group. She named this group "Transportation."

What group do the other pictures make?

Transportation

Trying the Skill

Use the pictures below to answer the
questions about sorting.

1. What groups can you make with
these pictures?

2. How are the things in each group alike?

3. What things in your classroom can
be sorted into groups?

About Money

We use coins and paper money to buy
things. Money comes in different amounts.
How much is a nickel worth?

In the United States paper money is made in Washington, D.C.

Our country's coins are made in places called mints. Philadelphia, Pennsylvania, has the biggest mint in the world.

1. Name some different kinds of coins.

2. How do you think we would pay for things if we didn't use coins or paper money?

Canada

Money in Other Countries

Every country in the world has its own money. The money in each country is different.

Mexico

United States

Brazil

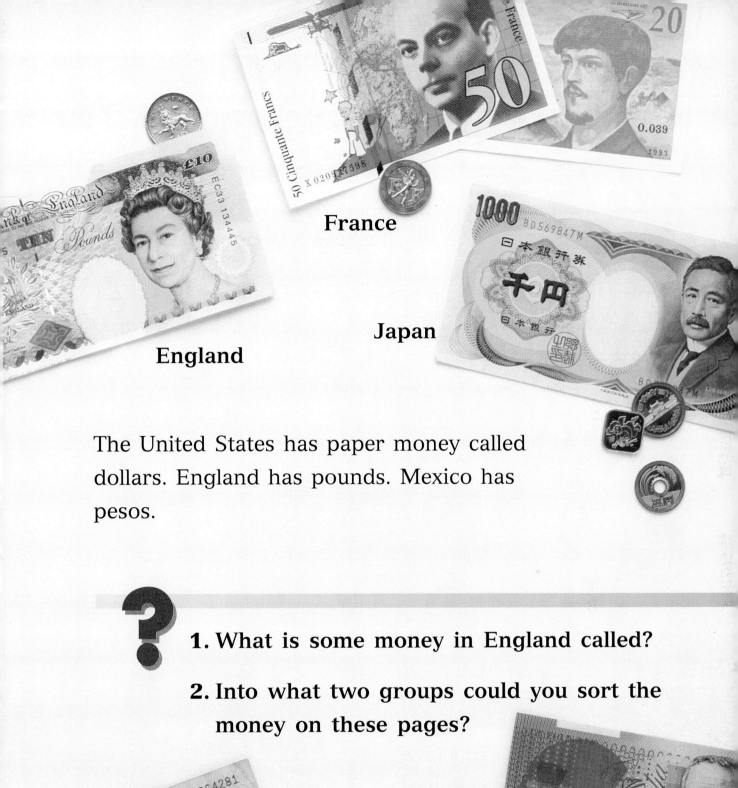

France

Japan

England

The United States has paper money called dollars. England has pounds. Mexico has pesos.

?

1. What is some money in England called?

2. Into what two groups could you sort the money on these pages?

Australia

Nigeria

STUDY SKILLS
Using Picture Graphs

A **picture graph** uses picture symbols to show numbers of things. The title tells you what the picture graph shows. This picture graph shows Pam's coins. Each picture symbol stands for one coin.

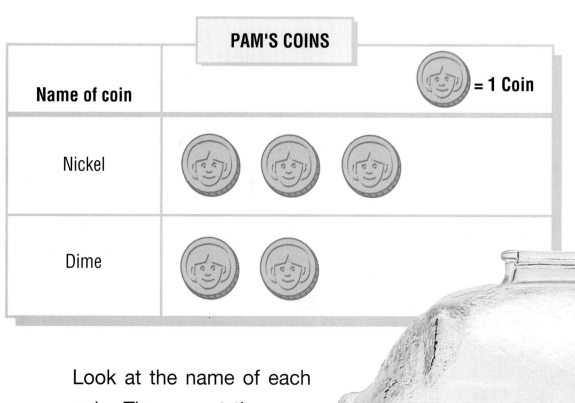

PAM'S COINS

Name of coin		= 1 Coin
Nickel	🪙 🪙 🪙	
Dime	🪙 🪙	

Look at the name of each coin. Then count the picture symbols next to the name. Pam has two dimes. How many nickels does she have?

Trying the Skill

Pam also has some money from other countries. Use this picture graph to answer the questions about her coins.

COINS FROM OTHER COUNTRIES

= 1 Coin

Country							
Brazil	🪙	🪙	🪙	🪙			
England	🪙	🪙	🪙				
Japan	🪙	🪙	🪙	🪙	🪙	🪙	🪙
Nigeria	🪙	🪙	🪙	🪙			

1. What does this picture graph show?
2. How many coins from England does Pam have?
3. Does Pam have more coins from Japan or from Brazil? How do you know?

Money's

Funny

by Mary Ann Hoberman

Money's funny
Don't you think?
Nickel's bigger than a dime;
So's a cent;
But when they're spent,
Dime is worth more
Every time.

Money's funny.

UNIT 3 REVIEW

Thinking About Words

Tell if these sentences are true or false. If the sentence is false, tell how to make it true.

1. **Wants** are the same for all people.
2. A place to live is called a **shelter**.
3. Things that are made or grown are **goods**.
4. **Needs** are things people can do without.
5. **Transportation** is how people or things move from one place to another.
6. A **service** is work done for others.
7. **Volunteers** are paid for their work.
8. A **job** is work that people do.

Thinking About Ideas

1. Why do people work?
2. What are four needs all people have?
3. Name some ways people help in your community.
4. Tell two ways that United States money is like money in other countries.

What job would you like to do when you grow up? Tell why.

Using Skills

Reviewing Using Picture Graphs

1. What does this picture graph show?
2. How many people work in an office?
3. How many people work in a store?
4. Where do most of the people work?

Where People In Our Families Work	Stands For One Worker
Factory	👤 👤 👤 👤 👤 👤
Store	👤 👤 👤 👤 👤
Office	👤 👤 👤 👤

Make Your Own!

- Make a picture graph. Show how many times you helped at home this week.
- Write the title at the top.
- List three jobs on the side of the graph.
- Draw a symbol of a house to show each time you helped.

Using Skills

Reviewing Sorting Things into Groups

Use these pictures to answer the questions about sorting.

1. Sort these pictures into two groups.

2. How are the things in each group alike?

3. How are the two groups different?

4. What could you add to each group?

UNIT REVIEW PROJECT

Make a Neighborhood of Shops

- Choose a store to make.
- Use a piece of paper to make windows. Glue them to a shoe box.
- Draw or cut out pictures that show goods or services in your store.
- Make a sign for your store.

Reading on Your Own

You can look for these books at your library.

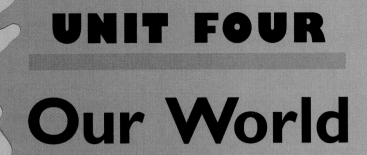

Key Words

plain

hill

mountain

lake

river

ocean

weather

season

continent

natural resource

Our Land and Water

Suppose you were flying high above the United States on a kite. You would see many kinds of land and water.

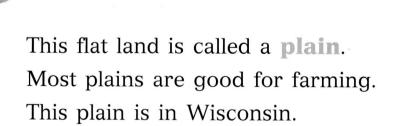

This flat land is called a **plain**. Most plains are good for farming. This plain is in Wisconsin.

These **hills** are in California. A hill is land higher than the land around it.

Mountains are the highest kind of land. This is Mount McKinley in Alaska. It is the tallest mountain in our country.

A lake is a body of water. It has land all around it. The city of Chicago is by Lake Michigan. Lakes can be big or small.

A river is a long body of water that flows across the land. This is a river in North Dakota.

Some rivers flow into lakes.
Other rivers flow into **oceans**.
An ocean is a very large body
of salt water. This is part of
the Atlantic Ocean.

1. Sort the words <u>plain</u>, <u>river</u>, <u>mountain</u>,
   and <u>lake</u> into two groups.

2. How are lakes and rivers different?

GEOGRAPHY SKILLS
Using Directions

North, east, south, and west are four **directions** on Earth. These directions can help you to find places on maps.

North is the direction toward the North Pole. South is the direction toward the South Pole. When you face north, east is to your right. What direction is to your left?

North

West   East

South

North

West   East

South

Trying the Skill

Use the map of the state of Kentucky to answer the questions below.

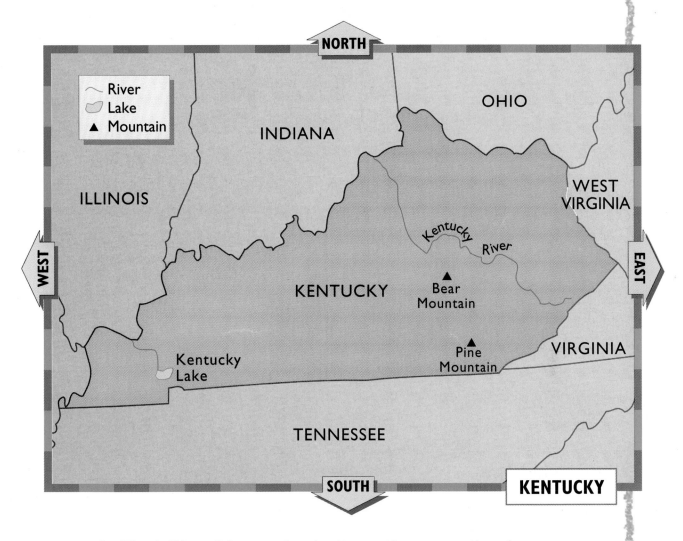

1. Find Pine Mountain. Is it north or south of Bear Mountain?
2. Name a state that is north of Kentucky.
3. In what ways can knowing about directions help you?

How's the Weather?

Beth lives in Indiana. Matt lives in California. Beth wanted to know if both states have the same **weather**. Weather is what it is like outside. Read their letters. What did Beth find out?

Dear Matt,

Yesterday it rained. Then it started to snow. Today it is sunny and cold. I made this snowman. Did it snow in California too?

Your friend,
Beth

Dear Beth,

It rained here on the day you got snow. The next day it was warm and sunny. Dad took me to the beach. Here is a sandman I made. I liked your snowman a lot!

Your friend,
Matt

Beth found out two places can have different weather at the same time. Some places in the North might be cold. On the same day, some places in the South might be warm.

In many places the weather changes as the **seasons** change. The seasons are spring, summer, fall, and winter. Here is what the seasons are like where Beth lives.

Spring

Summer

Winter

Fall

How do seasons in your community make a difference in the way you dress? How do they make a difference in the games you play?

1. Use the words <u>yesterday</u>, <u>today</u>, and <u>tomorrow</u> to tell about your weather.

2. How does your family enjoy the different seasons?

THINKING SKILLS
Putting Things in Order

When you put things in order, you tell what comes first, next, and last. You can put things in order by size or by time.

These pictures are in order by time. The first picture shows a clay ball. What does the next picture show? The last picture shows a clay snowman.

Trying the Skill

Put the pictures below in order by time.

1. Which picture comes first? Why?

2. Which picture comes next? Why?

3. Which picture comes last? Why?

4. How does putting these pictures in order help to tell a story?

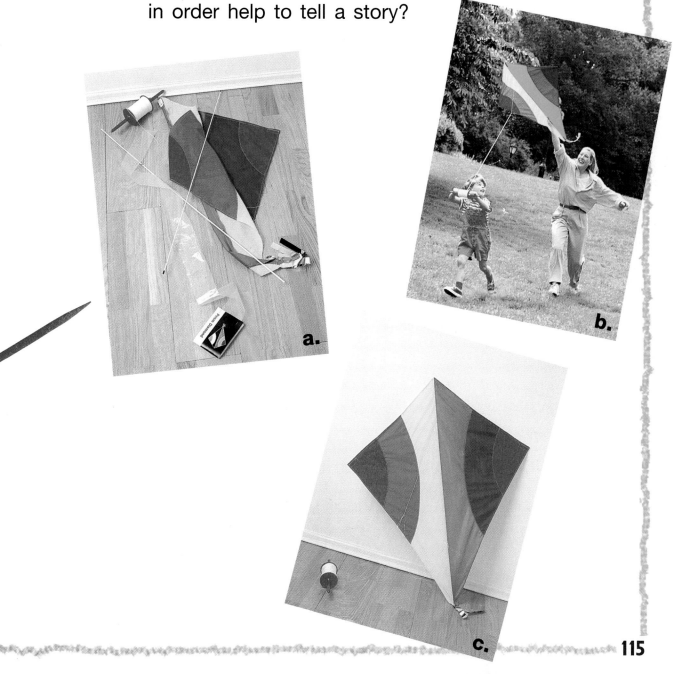

a.

b.

c.

Our Neighbors, Canada and Mexico

The United States has a neighbor country to the north. It is Canada. Mexico is our neighbor to the south.

THE UNITED STATES AND ITS NEIGHBORS

Taqtu lives in Canada. The winters are cold. The summers are warm.

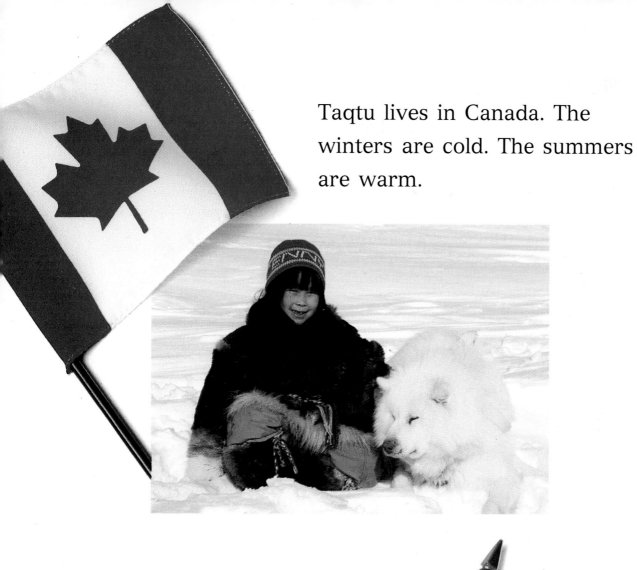

Carlos lives in Mexico. The weather there is warm and sunny most of the year.

NORTH AMERICA

PACIFIC OCEAN

ATLANTIC OCEAN

WEST

SOUTH AMERICA

PACIFIC OCEAN

ANTARCTICA

The United States, Mexico, and Canada are part of North America. North America is a **continent**. A continent is a very large body of land. There are seven continents on Earth.

Oceans are large bodies of water around the continents. Name the four oceans on Earth.

NORTH

ARCTIC OCEAN

EUROPE

ASIA

PACIFIC OCEAN

AFRICA

EAST

INDIAN OCEAN

ATLANTIC OCEAN

AUSTRALIA

ANTARCTICA

SOUTH

1. What two countries are neighbors of the United States?

2. Why is it important to learn about other countries?

Using Natural Resources

Natural resources are things in nature that people use. Air, water, and sunlight are natural resources. We need these resources to live.

Animals, plants, and soil are natural resources too. We use them to make food and other goods. Natural resources like coal, oil, and gas come from under the ground. They warm our homes.

Trees are another natural resource. Many things we use are made from trees.

All people need clean water. Here are ways
we use this natural resource.

1. What are three natural resources
   you use?

2. In what ways are natural resources
   important to us?

Caring for Our Natural Resources

"Welcome to Chain O'Lakes State Park," says Miss Hart. Miss Hart works in the park. This park is in Indiana.

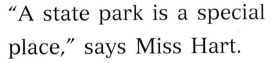

"A state park is a special
place," says Miss Hart.
"People come here to enjoy the trees.
They also enjoy other natural resources."

It is important to take care of Earth's
natural resources. If we use them up, we
will not have any left.

Here are some things you can do to help care for our Earth.

Help animals.

Keep our land, air, and water clean and beautiful.

Save things like these.
They can be made
into something new.

Use things over
and over.

1. How can you help care for
Earth's natural resources?

2. What might happen if we
don't take care of our
natural resources?

CITIZENSHIP
Making a Difference

CALIFORNIA

Los Angeles

Earth Niños

Yvette Ugalde wants Earth to be a clean place with lots of trees. She joined a club named Earth Niños. These English and Spanish words mean "Children for the Earth." The club is in Los Angeles, California.

Yvette and other children in the club collect empty cans.

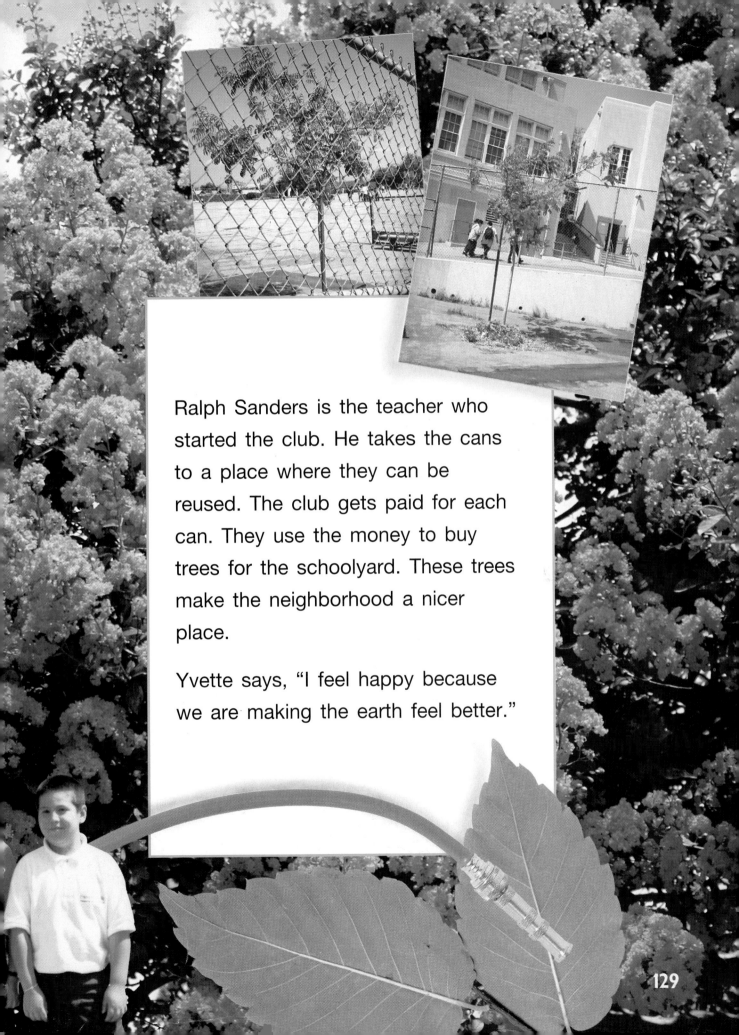

Ralph Sanders is the teacher who started the club. He takes the cans to a place where they can be reused. The club gets paid for each can. They use the money to buy trees for the schoolyard. These trees make the neighborhood a nicer place.

Yvette says, "I feel happy because we are making the earth feel better."

129

from

IT'S MY EARTH, TOO

HOW I CAN HELP THE
EARTH STAY ALIVE

BY
KATHLEEN KRULL

ILLUSTRATED BY
MELANIE HOPE GREENBERG

It's my Earth, too—
The Earth is where I live.
It gives me air to breathe,
water to drink,
soil for growing my food,
and animals to play with.
It's my Earth, too.

Oranges are juicy.

Carrots are crunchy.

Lettuce is munchy.

To get this food from the Earth to my stomach
takes rays of sunshine,

clean air blowing,

streams of rain,

and mounds of good soil.

That's a lot of the Earth's energy.

Shhhh—leaves whisper way above my head.
Squirrels run up and down the tall trees.
I wonder just how paper is made from trees.
The paper things I use every day
come from trees just like these.

Splish, splash. Water in my bath.

Drip, drop. Water from the faucet.

Water in the drinking fountain.

Hurray for water!

Without it we'd be always dirty, sticky, and thirsty.

That would make us crabby, mean, and sick.

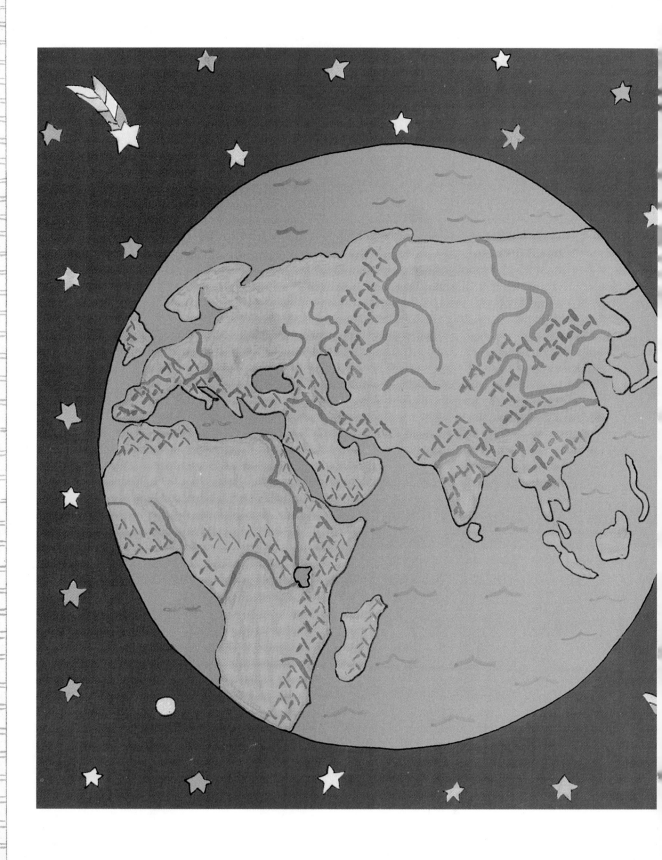

It's my Earth, too.

I hope that the air and water are always clean,

that the soil is always good,

that the animals stay alive,

that there is plenty of everything to go around.

UNIT 4 REVIEW

Thinking About Words

Match the words with the sentences below.

> plain   hill   mountain lake
> river   ocean   weather   season
> continents natural resources

1. I am the highest kind of land.
2. I am flat land.
3. I am a big body of salt water.
4. I am water surrounded by land.
5. We are trees, air, water, and sunlight.
6. There are seven of us on Earth.
7. I flow across the land.
8. I am not flat land or very high land.
9. I am spring, summer, fall, or winter.
10. I can be hot, cold, sunny, snowy, or rainy.

Thinking About Ideas

1. Tell how a river and an ocean are different.
2. What land and water are near you?
3. Tell how each season is different.

Tell about ways you can care for natural resources at school.

Using Skills

Reviewing Using Directions

Use the map to answer these questions.

1. Is Crater Lake to the north or south of Columbia River?

2. Is Powder River to the east or west of the Blue Mountains?

3. Are the Blue Mountains to the east or west of Crater Lake?

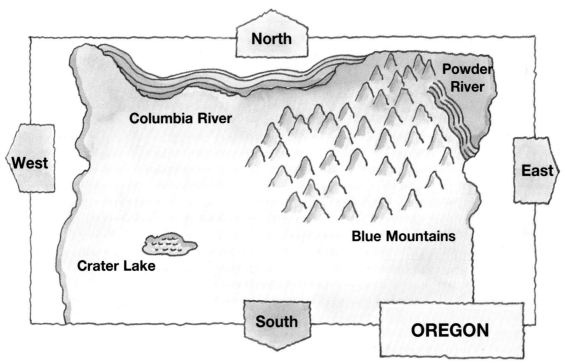

Make Your Own!

- Write each of the four directions on a different card.
- Tape the direction cards to your desk.
- Use the directions to tell where things are in your classroom.

Using Skills

Reviewing Putting Things in Order

Put these pictures in order by time.

1. Which picture comes first? Why?

2. Which picture comes next? Why?

3. Which picture comes last? Why?

4. How does putting these pictures in order help to tell a story?

a.

b.

c.

UNIT REVIEW PROJECT

Make a Poster of Resources

- Draw pictures of natural resources, such as sun, water, and trees.
- Make a poster to show how one of these natural resources is used.
- Write the name of the natural resource on the poster.

Reading on Your Own

You can look for these books at your library.

It Happened in America

Key Words

history

time line

Native Americans

settler

settlement

Pilgrims

Learning About the Past

What do you know about your past? Read this story about Kevin. See how he learned about his past.

My grandma has a quilt. It has patches in many colors.

"Each patch in the quilt tells about the past," Grandma told me.

"The white patch is from my wedding gown. It helps me remember the day I married your grandfather."

"The red patch is from a baseball cap. It was your Dad's cap when he was a boy," she said.

"This blue patch is a piece of your first blanket. It is six years old, just like you!"

Now I look at Grandma's quilt and remember stories about my family's past.

Our country has a past too. This past is called our **history**.

There are many ways to learn about our country's history. We can visit places. We can read books. How else can we learn about our past?

1. How did Kevin learn about his family's past?

2. How can we learn about our country's history?

STUDY SKILLS
Using Time Lines

A **time line** shows the order of things that happened. This time line shows what Kevin's grandmother did in one week. Each box on the time line is one day.

Grandmother's Week						
Sunday	**Monday**	**Tuesday**	**Wednesday**	**Thursday**	**Friday**	**Saturday**

Planted roses	Added patches to quilt	Worked at the library	Went shopping	Worked at the library	Celebrated Kevin's birthday	Went to zoo with Kevin

The time line starts on Sunday. On that day Kevin's grandmother planted roses. What did she do on Friday?

Trying the Skill

This time line tells about things that happened in Kevin's past. Each box on the time line is one year.

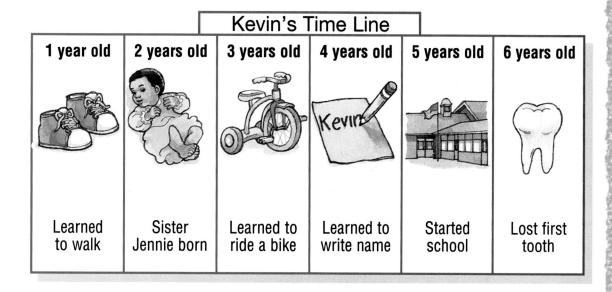

Kevin's Time Line

1 year old	2 years old	3 years old	4 years old	5 years old	6 years old
Learned to walk	Sister Jennie born	Learned to ride a bike	Learned to write name	Started school	Lost first tooth

Use the time line to answer these questions.

1. When did Kevin start to walk?

2. What happened when he was 2 years old?

3. How old was Kevin when he started school?

4. How would a time line help you remember things in your life?

The First People in America

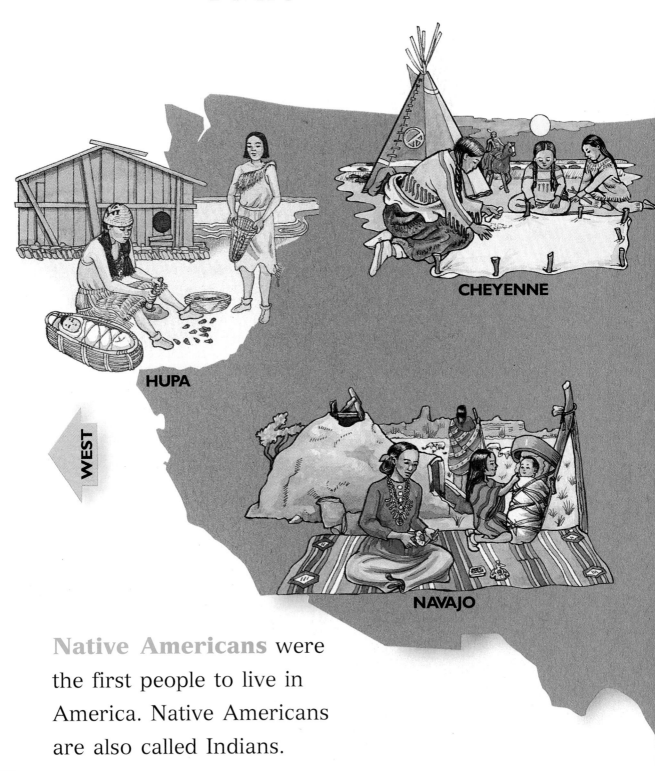

CHEYENNE

HUPA

WEST

NAVAJO

Native Americans were the first people to live in America. Native Americans are also called Indians.

There are many different groups of
Native Americans. This map shows
where some lived long ago. Today
some Native Americans live in the
same places. Find the Navajo
on the map.

NORTH

POTAWATOMI

WAMPANOAG

EAST

CHEROKEE

NATIVE AMERICAN
GROUPS

SOUTH

Deirdra's Scrapbook

my teacher

← me

Arizona

My name is Deirdra. I am
Navajo. We call ourselves
Diné. *Diné* means "the people"
in our language.

My family lives in Arizona. I am learning
about Navajo history. I am learning from
my family and my teacher.

In the past Navajo families lived in hogans. Hogans are one-room houses. They are made of logs, tree bark, and mud.

bark ↗

sheep →

Navajo families raised sheep. The sheep were used for food and wool. The wool made beautiful blankets and cloth.

These pictures show my community today.

Some Navajo still live in hogans. We still do some things as in the past. I like knowing the Navajo have a special history.

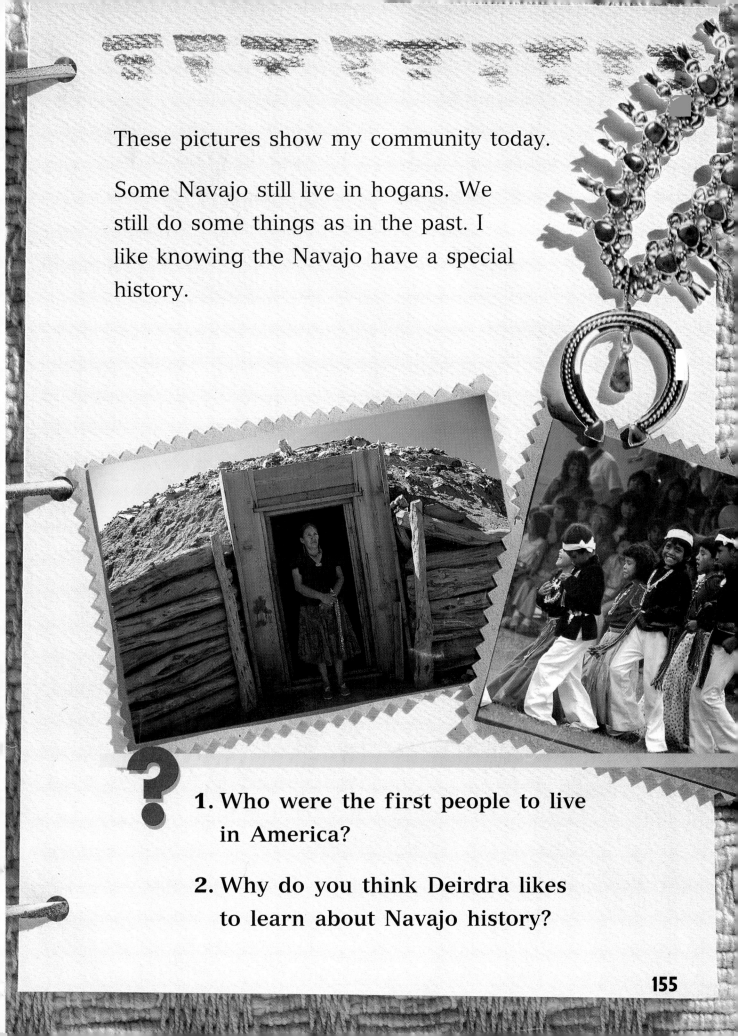

1. Who were the first people to live in America?

2. Why do you think Deirdra likes to learn about Navajo history?

Christopher Columbus Comes to America

"Land! Land!" a sailor called out to his captain. The captain was Christopher Columbus.

Columbus and his men sailed across the Atlantic Ocean long ago. They sailed from Spain. Spain is a country in Europe.

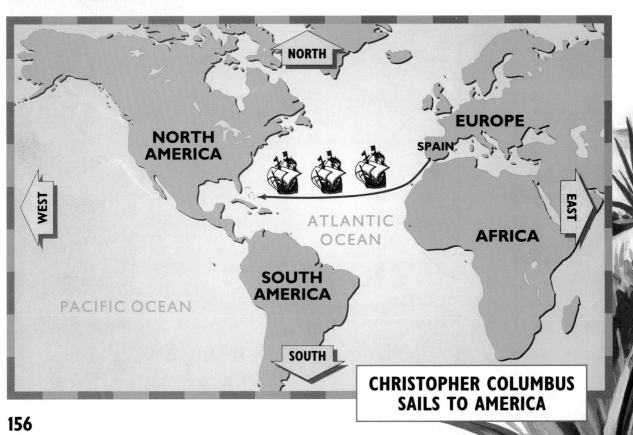

CHRISTOPHER COLUMBUS SAILS TO AMERICA

Columbus's ships were named the *Niña,* the *Pinta,* and the *Santa María.* Columbus hoped to find gold and riches in Asia. Instead he landed on an island in North America.

Native Americans called the Taino lived on the island. The Taino welcomed Columbus and his men.

The Taino gave the men plants and birds.
They also gave them tomatoes and corn.
The sailors had never seen these foods
before.

Columbus went back to Spain. He took back the birds and plants the Taino had given him.

Columbus made three more trips to North America. He never found much gold. But he did find a place that people in Europe did not know about.

1. Who lived on the island where Columbus landed?

2. Why do you think Columbus took birds and plants back to Spain?

STUDY SKILLS
Finding the Main Idea

The **main idea** tells what a story is about. Finding the main idea helps you to understand what you read.

Read this story to find the main idea.

Christopher Columbus wanted to learn about the world. He looked at maps. He asked people about the places they had been.

Sometimes the main idea of a story is the first sentence. The main idea in this story is that Christopher Columbus wanted to learn about the world. The other sentences tell what he did to learn about the world.

Trying the Skill

Read this story to find the main idea.

The Taino were good boat builders. They built large boats called canoes. The Taino sailed many miles in their canoes.

1. What is the main idea of this story?
2. How can knowing the main idea be helpful?

A Place Called Santa Fe

Settlers from many countries came to North America after Columbus. People who move from one place to live in another are settlers.

Settlers from Spain moved to Mexico. Some moved to what is now New Mexico. They built **settlements**. A settlement is a small community built by settlers. One settlement became Santa Fe.

Native Americans lived near Santa Fe. The Spanish called them "Pueblos." Their homes were called pueblos too.

Santa Fe is one of our country's oldest cities.

Visiting a pueblo

1. What is a settler?

2. What places in your community were built long ago?

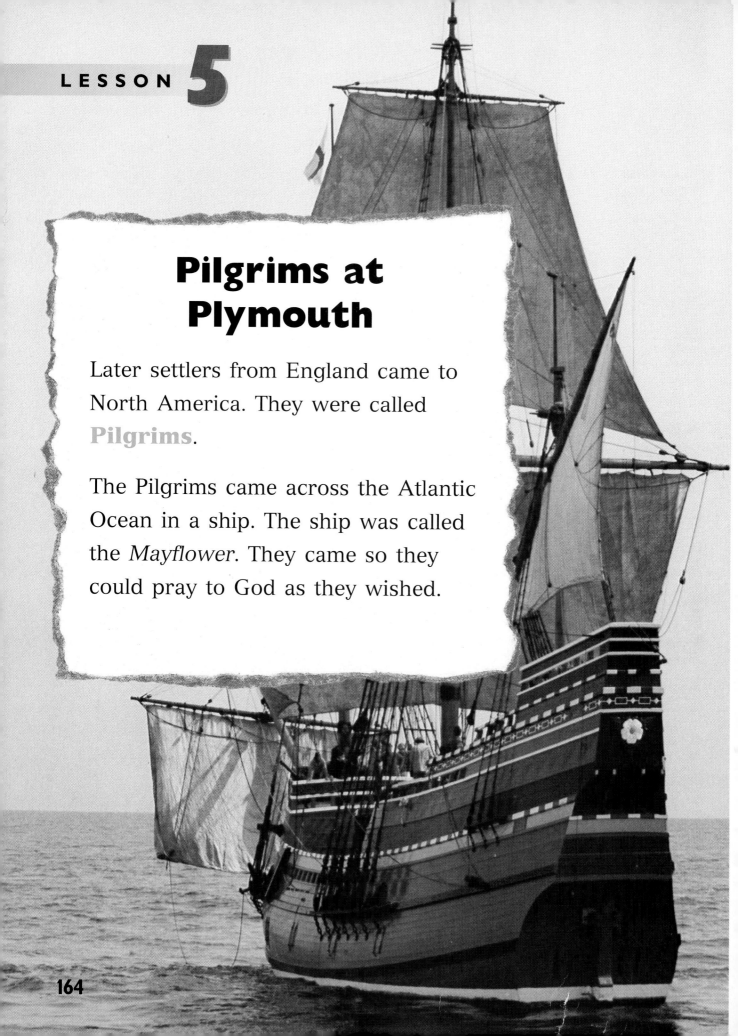

Pilgrims at Plymouth

Later settlers from England came to North America. They were called **Pilgrims**.

The Pilgrims came across the Atlantic Ocean in a ship. The ship was called the *Mayflower*. They came so they could pray to God as they wished.

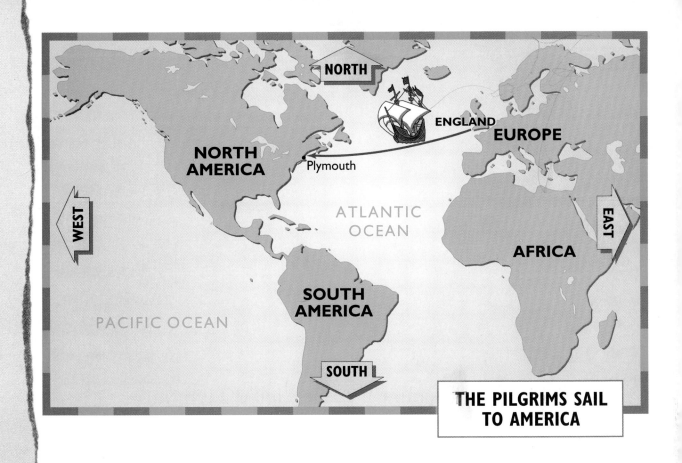

THE PILGRIMS SAIL
TO AMERICA

The trip was hard for the Pilgrims.
There were storms at sea. Many people
became sick.

One day the Pilgrims heard "Land ho!"
They had reached North America.
It was winter.

The Pilgrims built a town called Plymouth in what is now Massachusetts.

In the spring they met the Wampanoag Indians. The Wampanoag sent Squanto to help the Pilgrims. Squanto showed them how to fish, hunt, and grow food.

By fall the fields were full of food. The Pilgrims decided to have a special meal. They asked the Wampanoag to join them.

The Pilgrims gave thanks to God. They now had food, strong homes, and good friends.

1. How did Squanto help the Pilgrims?

2. Why do you think the Pilgrims needed the Wampanoag's help?

A Country of Many People

More and more people came to America. They came from many countries in Europe.

People came to find work. They wanted to start a new life. They came to pray to God in their own way. They wanted to be free.

Baltimore Historical Society

The Granger Collection

Some people did not come to America by choice. These people were from Africa. Many Africans were forced to be slaves. Slaves worked without pay. They dreamed of being free. That day came after a long time.

Many new people moved to America.
They built homes. They raised families.
They worked hard.

Towns and cities grew. Soon there was a
new country. The new country became
the United States of America.

The Granger Collection

Chin Yee Hee was born in China. He and other people from China planned and built railroads. These railroads joined towns and cities across the United States.

Edward Corsi came to the United States
when he was a boy. His family came from
Italy by boat. The United States was the
country of their dreams.

The first thing Edward saw was the Statue
of Liberty. He remembers people holding
their babies high so they could see it.

Today people are still coming to the United States. They come from many countries.

The United States is still the land of dreams.

1. Tell reasons why people came to America long ago.

2. Why do you think people come to the United States today?

CITIZENSHIP
Making a Difference

NEW YORK

New York City

Miss Janey and class

Welcome to New York City

Janey Markon is a teacher in New York City. She works with "Project Reach Youth." She helps children from all over the world who move to New York City.

"Miss Janey" knows that moving to a new place is not easy. There is so much to learn.

Taking the bus

Jelen

Miss Janey teaches the children English. She shows them how to use money and get around on a bus. She says, "The more that children know about a new place, the sooner they will feel at home."

Jelen DeCastro is one of Miss Janey's students. He is from the Dominican Republic. He loves New York pizza!

WHAT WAS

"What was it like
when you were as old as I am now?"
a little girl asked her mother.
"Well, when I went to bed,"
her mother said,
"the room was dark
the clocks ticked
grown-ups talked downstairs
the stars shone in the sky
and I could hear the wind in the trees
    outside
before I hugged my mother good night
the way you do now."

BY CHARLOTTE ZOLOTOW
ILLUSTRATED BY MELISSA SWEET

UNIT 5 REVIEW

Thinking About Words

Choose the word or words that best tell about each sentence.

> **history**   **Pilgrims**   **settlers**   **settlement**
> **Native Americans**

1. These people are also called Indians.
2. This is a small community built by settlers.
3. These are people who move from one place to live in a different place.
4. This is our country's past.
5. These people came to North America on the *Mayflower*.

Thinking About Ideas

1. Who were the first Americans?
2. How did North America change after Columbus came here?
3. Why did the Pilgrims have a special meal?
4. Why did people come to America long ago?

 What is your favorite story from our country's past? Tell why.

Using Skills

Reviewing Using Time Lines

Use the time line to answer the questions.

The Pilgrim's First Year

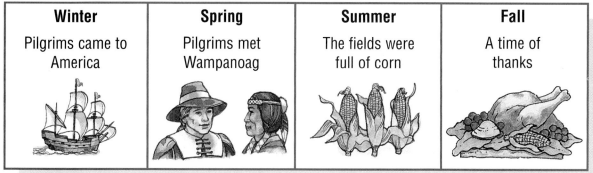

Winter	Spring	Summer	Fall
Pilgrims came to America	Pilgrims met Wampanoag	The fields were full of corn	A time of thanks

1. What happened in the fall?

2. What happened in the spring?

3. When did the Pilgrims come to America?

Make Your Own!

My Week

Sunday	Monday	Tuesday	Wednesday	Thursday	Friday	Saturday
saw Grandfather	played soccer	class trip	made paper boats	saw a movie	went to the library	played with Sam

- Write each day of the week at the top of a different sheet of paper.
- Draw and write what you did that day.
- Put the pictures in order. Start with Sunday.
- Tape your time line together.

Using Skills

Reviewing Finding the Main Idea

Read this story to find the main idea.

People from many places built communities in America. They built homes and farms. They worked in schools. They built railroads.

1. What is the main idea of this story?
2. Which three pictures tell about the main idea?
3. Which picture does not show the main idea? Why?

a.

b.

c.

d.

UNIT REVIEW PROJECT

Make a History Storybook

- Choose a person or group from history, such as the Pilgrims.
- Draw three pictures about the person or group.
- Write a sentence under each picture.
- Punch a hole in each page.
- Tie your book together with a piece of yarn.

Reading on Your Own

You can look for these books at your library.

UNIT SIX

Americans Celebrate

Key Words

holiday

calendar

celebrate

Holidays for Presidents

Holidays are special days. On some holidays we remember important people. On others we remember something that happened.

Presidents' Day is a holiday in February. On that day we remember George Washington. We also remember another President, named Abraham Lincoln.

George Washington

The Granger Collection

George Washington's Home

Washington Monument

Long ago America was not free. It was ruled by the country of England.

Americans fought a war to become free from England. George Washington became our first President. He is called the "Father of our Country."

Abraham Lincoln was President long after George Washington. When Lincoln was a child, he was poor. He worked hard to become a leader.

Lincoln led our country during another war. He helped to free African Americans who were slaves.

Abraham Lincoln

Abraham Lincoln was a strong leader. We remember him as fair. He is called "Honest Abe."

Abraham Lincoln's Home

Lincoln Memorial

1. Who do we remember on Presidents' Day?

2. How are George Washington and Abraham Lincoln alike?

STUDY SKILLS
Using Calendars

Calendars are charts that show the months of a year. They show the weeks in a month. They also show the days in a week. Calendars show holidays too.

This calendar shows the month of February. Each block on the calendar is one day. How many days are in this month?

FEBRUARY

SUNDAY	MONDAY	TUESDAY	WEDNESDAY	THURSDAY	FRIDAY	SATURDAY
						1
2	3	4	5	6	7	8
9	10	11	12	13	14 Valentine's Day	15
16	17 Presidents' Day	18	19	20	21	22
23	24	25	26	27	28	

JUNE

SUNDAY	MONDAY	TUESDAY	WEDNESDAY	THURSDAY	FRIDAY	SATURDAY
1	2	3	4	5	6	7
8	9	10	11	12	13	14 Flag Day
15 Father's Day	16	17	18	19	20	21
22	23	24	25	26	27	28
29	30					

Trying the Skill

Use the calendar above to answer these questions.

1. How many days are in this month?

2. What day of the week is June 14? What is the name of that day?

3. On which day is Father's Day?

4. How is a calendar useful?

Special Days for Our Country

Americans **celebrate** many holidays.
We celebrate by doing something special.

We celebrate Independence Day on July 4.
We remember July 4 in 1776. On that day
the United States said it was free
from England.

Independence Day is our country's birthday. We celebrate with parades. We celebrate with fireworks. We show that we are proud to be Americans.

JULY

Columbus Day is in October. On that day we remember when Christopher Columbus came to America.

Thanksgiving Day is in November. We remember the special meal the Pilgrims and the Wampanoag ate together.

In January we remember Martin Luther King, Jr. He worked to make laws fair for all Americans.

JANUARY

1. Name two holidays for our country. Why do we celebrate them?

2. Why do people celebrate holidays?

THINKING SKILLS
Making Predictions

When you tell what you think will happen next, you are making a **prediction**. Read the story below. Make a prediction about what will happen next.

Betsy Ross liked to sew. President George Washington wanted a flag for our new country. He knew Betsy Ross could sew.

What do you think George Washington did? Did you make the prediction that George Washington asked Betsy Ross to make our flag? Why?

Trying the Skill

Read the story below. Then answer the questions.

Betsy Ross cut out the pieces to make a flag. She sewed the red and white stripes together. She sewed on the stars. Then George Washington came to see the flag.

1. What do you think happened next? Tell how you came up with your prediction.
2. How does making predictions help you in school?

Special Days for Families

Families celebrate many special days.

They celebrate the day a new baby is born.

Families also celebrate when a child finishes school.

196

A wedding is another special day.

Sometimes all the people in a family get together. This is a way to remember the past.

Some families share other special days too.
These holidays are celebrated every year.

Christmas is celebrated on December 25.

Hanukkah is usually celebrated in December. It lasts eight days.

Kwanzaa begins on December 26. It ends on January 6.

Chinese New Year is celebrated in January or February. The holiday lasts three days.

Three Kings Day is celebrated on January 6.

1. Do all families celebrate the same special days? Tell why or why not.

2. How will you celebrate your next special day? Make a prediction.

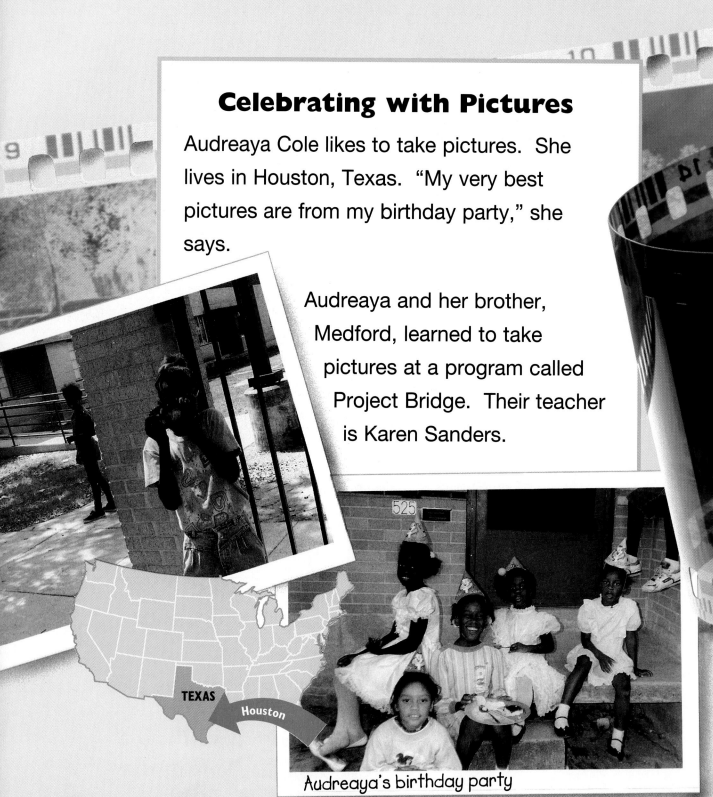

Celebrating with Pictures

Audreaya Cole likes to take pictures. She lives in Houston, Texas. "My very best pictures are from my birthday party," she says.

Audreaya and her brother, Medford, learned to take pictures at a program called Project Bridge. Their teacher is Karen Sanders.

TEXAS

Houston

Audreaya's birthday party

Audreaya taking pictures

The children get cameras and film to take home. They take pictures of their neighborhood and their families.

Miss Sanders picks the best pictures for a photography show. Families and friends come to the show.

"I felt so good when I saw my pictures at that show," says Medford.

Celebrating Spring

People around the world celebrate the start of spring.

In the United States, some children roll Easter eggs on the White House Lawn.

Some people in China celebrate a holiday called Ching Ming. People clean house, plant flowers, and remember their families.

202

On May 1 some children in England sing and dance around a Maypole. They are celebrating trees in spring.

In Spain some people go to a Spring Fair. They put up tents for parties. They ride in parades on horses.

1. Name two ways that people celebrate spring. How are these ways alike and different?

2. Why do you think people in many places like to celebrate spring?

Symbols Say U.S.A.!

Many symbols stand for the United States. These symbols make us think of our country.

The Statue of Liberty is a symbol. It stands for hope. It also stands for freedom and friendship. The statue is in New York Harbor.

The Liberty Bell is a symbol. It stands for freedom. The Liberty Bell rang when the United States became a country. You can see this symbol in Philadelphia, Pennsylvania.

The bald eagle is another symbol. It stands for our country. You can see this symbol on some of our country's money.

The American flag is an important symbol of our country. It has 13 stripes and 50 stars. Each star stands for a state. The flag is red, white, and blue.

white

CRAYON

THE PLEDGE OF ALLEGIANCE

I pledge allegiance to the flag of the United States of America and to the Republic for which it stands, one Nation under God, indivisible, with liberty and justice for all.

We say the *Pledge of Allegiance*. It honors our flag and our country. We honor our flag on Flag Day, June 14.

1. Name two symbols of the United States.

2. Why do you think we have symbols for our country?

CLOSE With A Song

You're a Grand Old Flag

Words and Music
by George M. Cohan

You're a grand old flag, you're a high-fly-ing flag;

And for-ev-er in peace may you wave; _____

You're the em-blem of the land I love,

The home of the free and the brave. _____

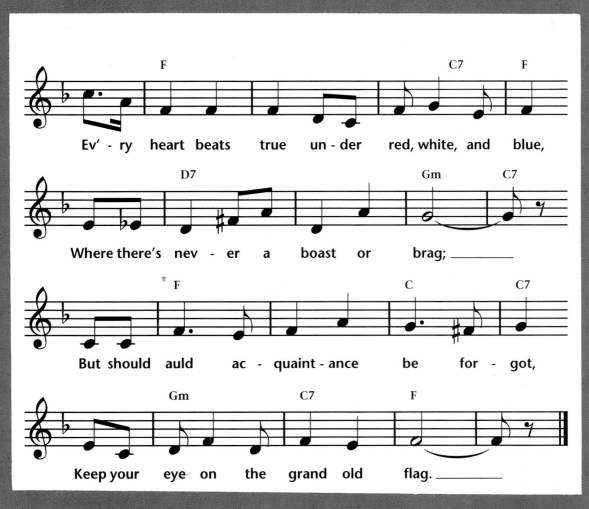

UNIT 6 REVIEW

Thinking About Words

Use these words to finish the sentences.

| calendar | holiday | celebrate |
| prediction | | |

1. A special day is a _____.
2. A _____ is a chart that shows the days, weeks, and months of the year.
3. Americans _____ many holidays each year.
4. You make a _____ when you tell what you think will happen next.

Thinking About Ideas

1. Name two holidays that honor our past.
2. What special day is important to your family?
3. How do some people celebrate spring?
4. Name two symbols that stand for freedom.

Which special days do you like? Tell why.

Using Skills

Reviewing Using Calendars

1. Which month does this calendar show?
2. How many days are in this month?
3. What special day is celebrated on May 29?
4. When is Mother's Day?

MAY

Sunday	Monday	Tuesday	Wednesday	Thursday	Friday	Saturday
	1	2	3	4	5	6
7	8	9	10	11	12	13
14 Mother's Day	15	16	17	18	19	20
21	22	23	24	25	26	27
28	29 Memorial Day	30	31			

Make Your Own!

- Make a calendar with seven squares across and six squares down.
- Write the name of a month.
- Write the days of the week.
- Write the numbers for the days in the month.
- Add any special days in the month.

JUNE

Sunday	Monday	Tuesday	Wednesday	Thursday	Friday	Saturday
				1	2	3
4	5	6	7	8	9	10
11	12	13	14	15	16	17
18	19	20	21	22	23	24
25	26	27	28	29	30	

Using Skills

Reviewing Making Predictions

Read to predict what happens next.

Today is Sally's birthday. Sally's mother has a present for her. It is hidden in a closet. Sally's mother sees Sally about to open the closet.

1. Make a prediction about what could happen if Sally opens the closet.
2. What do you think Sally's mother will say?
3. What do you think Sally will say?

Make a Card for a Special Day

- Fold a sheet of paper in half.
- Draw a picture about a special day on the front of your card.
- Add pictures inside your card.
- Send your card to someone special.

Reading on Your Own

You can look for these books at your library.

THE UNITED STATES

RUSSIA

ARCTIC OCEAN

ALASKA

CANADA

Juneau ★

PACIFIC OCEAN

CANADA

★ Olympia
WASHINGTON

Helena ★
MONTANA

★ Salem

OREGON

IDAHO

★ Boise

WYOMING

WEST

PACIFIC OCEAN

NEVADA

★ Carson City

★ Sacramento

Great Salt Lake

★ Salt Lake City

Cheyenne ★

UTAH

Denver ★

COLORADO

CALIFORNIA

★ Santa Fe

ARIZONA

NEW MEXICO

★ Phoenix

Honolulu ★
HAWAII

PACIFIC OCEAN

MEXICO

ARCTIC OCEAN

NORTH AMERICA

ATLANTIC OCEAN

PACIFIC OCEAN

WEST

SOUTH AMERICA

ANTARCTICA

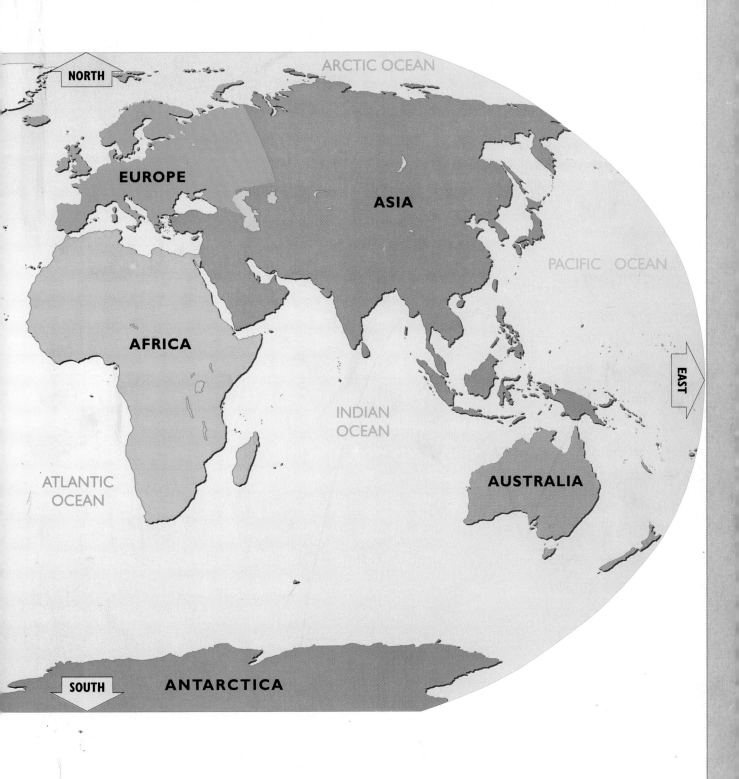

NORTH

ARCTIC OCEAN

EUROPE

ASIA

PACIFIC OCEAN

AFRICA

EAST

INDIAN
OCEAN

ATLANTIC
OCEAN

AUSTRALIA

SOUTH

ANTARCTICA

Dictionary of GEOGRAPHIC WORDS

HILL Land that is higher than the land around it, but lower than a mountain.

PLAIN Flat land.

LAKE Body of water with land all around it.

MOUNTAIN Highest kind of land.

RIVER Long body of water that flows across the land.

OCEAN Very big body of salt water.

PICTURE GLOSSARY

alike

These kittens look **alike**.

(page 50)

calendar

This **calendar** shows the month of May. (page 188)

celebrate

I will **celebrate** my seventh birthday. (page 190)

chart

The **chart** shows who won the game. (page 58)

citizen

Lara is a **citizen** of this country. So is Ken. (page 63)

community

There are many neighborhoods in this **community**. (page 16)

continent

North America is a **continent** on Earth. (page 118)

country

The United States of America is our **country**. (page 24)

different

My hat is **different** from Bill's. (page 50)

directions

North, south, east, and west are **directions** on a map. (page 108)

Earth

We call our world **Earth**. It has land and water. (page 27)

family

There are two children in Lola's **family**. (page 44)

goods
My dress, book, and this orange are **goods**. (page 76)

group
Fran and her friends are a **group**. (page 48)

hill
It is fun to ride a bike down a **hill**. (page 105)

history
The story of America's past is called **history**. (page 147)

holiday
Flag Day is a **holiday** in June. (page 184)

job
My brother has a **job** in a store. (page 74)

lake
Water in a **lake** is often very cold. (page 106)

law
It is a **law** to cross with the green light. (page 54)

main idea
The **main idea** tells what a story is about. (page 160)

map
You can find my school on this **map**. (page 9)

map key
A **map key** can help you read a map. (page 22)

mountain
A **mountain** may have snow all year long.
(page 105)

Native Americans

The first people to live in America are called Indians or **Native Americans**. (page 150)

natural resource

Water is a **natural resource** that people and animals use. (page 120)

needs

Food, clothing, shelter, and love are **needs**. (page 78)

neighborhood

People live, work, and play in my **neighborhood**. (page 7)

ocean

Many ships sail across the **ocean**. (page 107)

order

Debby put the books in **order** from A to Z. (page 114)

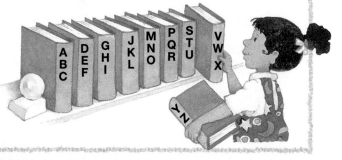

PICTURE Glossary

picture graph
This **picture graph** shows how many red and blue crayons I have. (page 94)

Pilgrims
Pilgrims came to North America on the *Mayflower.* (page 164)

plain
Our farm is on flat land called a **plain.** (page 104)

prediction
I made a **prediction** that it would rain. (page 194)

President
George Washington was our first **President.** (page 63)

river
Boats, people, fish, and plants share a **river.** (page 106)

rule

It is a **rule** to raise your hand if you have a question. (page 52)

season

Spring is a **season**. (page 112)

service

My dad is a firefighter. He does a **service** for others. (page 76)

settlement

The Pilgrims built a **settlement** at Plymouth. (page 162)

settlers

Settlers built schools and farms. (page 162)

shelter

Our home is my family's **shelter**. (page 78)

sort

I like to **sort** things into groups. (page 88)

state

Louisiana is a **state** in our country. (page 24)

time line

Marcy's **time line** tells when she learned to swim.
(page 148)

transportation

A school bus is a kind of **transportation**. (page 85)

volunteer

Jane's mom is a **volunteer** at the library. (page 77)

vote

Citizens can **vote** for a President. (page 60)

wants

This bike and skates are **wants**. (page 80)

weather

Sunshine brings warm **weather**. (page 110)

index

CREDITS

Cover: Pentagram

Maps: Geosystems

Illustrations: Ellen Appleby: pp 124-127, 202-203; Yvette Banek: pp 38, 68, 70, 98, 100, 138, 139(t), 140, 210, 212; Nan Brooks: pp 82-83; Randy Chewning: pp 84-87, 88, 89; Luisa DiAugusta: pp 86-97; Eldon Doty: pp 74, 75, 76, 77; Alyssa Gallo: pp 120-121; Michael Grejniec: pp 66-67; Meryl Henderson: pp 148, 149, 168, 169, 170, 171, 172, 179(t), 180; Brian Karas: pp 48, 49, 56-57; Cheryl Kirk Knoll: pp 150-151; Alan Leiner: pp 165, 166, 167; Claude Martinot: pp 53; Karen Minot: pp R6-R7; Hima Pamoedjo: pp 21(m), 48-49, 69(t), 94, 95, 99(t), 191, 192, 193, 211(t); Rebecca Perry: pp 39(t), 40; Roz Schanzer: pp 30-37(border); Jerry Smath: pp R8-R15; Melissa Sweet: pp 176-177; Peggy Tagel: pp 23, 42-43, 72-73, 102-103, 142-143, 182-183; Mary Thelen: pp 208-209; Steve Sullivan: pp 54, 58, 59; Robert Van Nutt: pp 156-157, 158-159, 160, 161; Nina Wallace: pp 8, 9, 20-21, 22, 23

Thank you to all the children who contributed their work, including Alyssa Gallo, Brentin Gultz, Molly Mc Fadden, Paul Mitchell, Christopher Mitchell, Rita Munifo, and Mrs. Struzik's first grade class in Netcong, New Jersey.

PHOTOGRAPHY CREDITS: All photographs are by the Macmillan/McGraw-Hill School Division (MMSD) except as noted below.

Cover and I: Bob Esparza for MMSD. iii t.l. Grant Heilman/Grant Heilman Photography, Inc.; b.l. Jim Levin for MMSD. iv: t. Key Photos; m. Francis Westfield for MMSD; b. Runk Schoenberger/Grant Heilman Photography, Inc. v: t. Francis Westfield for MMSD; m. Bob Daemmrich/Stock Boston, Inc.; b. Uniphoto, Inc. vi: b. Francis Westfield for MMSD. x: t. Ric Ergenbright; b. Tom McCarthy/National Stock Network. x-xi: Elizebth Wolf. xi: t.r. Joseph H. Bailey; m. Breton Littlehales; b.r. Joseph H. Bailey. Unit 1 2: Bob Jones, Jr./Liaison International. 3: l. Joe Viesti/Viesti Associates, Inc.; t.r. Tony Stone Images.

10: l. David Meunch; r. John Feingersh/The Stock Market. 11: Lionel Delevingne/Stock Boston, Inc.

13: James Levin. 14-15: Andy Sacks for MMSD. 15: l. Andy Sacks for MMSD; r. Phil Degginger/Bruce Coleman. 16: Loren Irvin. 17: Superstock.

20: Albert J. Gordon/Profiles West. 22: t.l. Grant Heilman/Grant Heilman Photography, Inc.; b.l. C.J. Allen/Stock Boston. 25: Richard Hirneisen for MMSD. 26: r., b.r. R. Larry Lefever/Grant Heilman Photography, Inc. 28: t.l. Margarette Mead/The Image Bank; t.m. Ken Karp for MMSD; t. Bruce Caines for MMSD; t.r. E.R. Degginger/Bruce Coleman, Inc.; m.r., b.m. Scott Harvey for MMSD; b.r. Titus Kana for MMSD; r. L.D. Gordon/The Image Bank; l. Mulvehill/The Image Works. 29: t.r. Ken Karp for MMSD; t. Ed Bock/The stock Market; b.r. Karen Ann Wilson/Natural Selection; b.m. Gamma Liaison; m.l. Bill Waltzen for MMSD; b.l. Ken Karp for MMSD. Unit 2 42: t.l. Terry Farmer/Tony Stone Images; b.l. Lori Adamski Peek/Tony Stone Images. 43: l. The Granger Collection. 44-45: Francis Westfield for MMSD. 46-47: l. Superstock. 47: r. Elliott Smith. 48: b.l. Don Klumpp; b.r. Paul Miller/Black Star; r. Jim Levin for MMSD. 49: t.r. Wayne Eastep/Tony Stone Image; t.l. Lawrence Migdale; b. Jim Levin for MMSD.

51: t. Tomas del Ano/Adstock Photos. 52: Jim Levin for MMSD. 53: Francis Westfield for MMSD. 54: Jim Levin for MMSD. 55: t.r. Sam Sargent/Liaison International; m.r. C. Podias/FPG International; b.r. Patrick Eden/The Image Bank; m. Jim Levin for MMSD. 60-62: Jim Levin for MMSD. 63: Cynthia Johnson/Gamma-Liaison. 64: l. Key Photos; b.r. Michael S. Yamashita/The Stock House, Ltd. 65: t. Karen Kasmauski/Woodfin Camp & Associates. 71: Monica Stevenson for MMSD. Unit 3 72: t.l. Jeff Dunn/The Picture Cube; t.r. Bob Abraham/The Stock Market; m.r. Michael Heron/Woodfin Camp for MMSD. 73: b.l. Eric Roth/The Picture Cube; t. Juan Pablo Lira/The Image Bank. 74-75: Francis Westfield. 76: b. David Young Wolff/Photo Edit; t. Thomas Del Brase/The Stock Market. 77: l. Charles Gupton/Tony Stone International; r. Francis Westfield for MMSD. 78: l. Francis Westfield for MMSD; r. Ulf Sjostedt/FPG International. 79-81: Francis Westfield for MMSD. 84: Courtesy of The Oshkosh Public Museum. 85: l. Beringer-Dratch/The Picture Cube; r. John Terence Turner/FPG. 86: t. Tony Stone Worldwide; b. Alan Pitcairn/Grant Heilman. 87: t. Peter Cole/Bruce Coleman; b. Peter Gridley/FPG International. 88, 90: Francis Westfield for MMSD. 91: t. Kay Chernush/The Image Bank; b. Cameramann International. 92-94: Francis Westfield for MMSD. 101: Monica Stevenson for MMSD. Unit 4 104: b., t.r. Francis Westfield for MMSD; m. Tom Bean/The Stock Market. 105: Hans Wendler/The Image Bank; b. Ken Graham/Tony Stone Images. 106: t.l. Berenholtz/The Stock Market; m.r. David Weintraub/Photo Researchers; b.l. James P. Blair/National Geographic Society Image Collection; t.r. Francis Westfield for MMSD. 107: t. S.R. maglione/Photo Researchers; b. Runk Schoenberger/Grant Heilman. 108: b. Francis Westfield for MMSD; t. Runk Schoenberger/Grant Heilman. 110: t.r. Francis Westfield for MMSD; b.r. Bill Frantz/Tony Stone Images. 110-111: bkgnd. Francis Westfield for MMSD. 111: Francis Westfield for MMSD. 112: l. Jan Halaska/Photo Researchers; r. Jan Halaska/Photo Researchers. 112-113: Francis Westfield for MMSD. 113: Jan Halaska/Photo Researchers. 114-115: Francis Westfield for MMSD. 117: t.l. Francis Westfield for MMSD; b.r. Francis Westfield for MMSD; b.l. Will & Deni McIntyre/Tony Stone Images; t.r. M. Macri/Masterfile. 120-121: bkgnd. Francis Westfield for MMSD. 120: l. David R. Frazier Photo Library. 121: r. Renee Lynn/Photo Researchers. 122: m.l., b.l. Francis Westfield for MMSD; t.m. Gary Buss/FPG International; b.m. Don Smetzer/Tony Stone Images. 122-123: Francis Westfield for MMSD. 123: t.l. John Mead/SPL/Photo Researchers; t.r. Dennis Brack/Balck Star; b.r. Suan Pfannmuller/Midwestock. 124: l. Francis Westfield for MMSD; r. Cathlyn Melloan/Tony Stone Images. 125: r. Vanessa Vick/Photo Researchers, Inc. 126: Francis Westfield for MMSD. 127: t.l. Michael Krasowitz/FPG International; r. Francis Westfield for MMSD. 128-129: Grant Heilman Photography. 128: m. Monica Stevenson for MMSD; b.r., t.r. Ralph W. Sanders for MMSD; t.m. Monica Stevenson for MMSD. 129: t.l., t.r. Ralph W. Sanders for MMSD; b.r. Monica Stevenson for MMSD. 141: Monica Stevenson for MMSD. Unit 5 1452: t. The Granger Collection; m.r. Mark E. Gibson; t. The Granger Collection. 143: m. Uniphoto, Inc. 145: t.l. courtesy C.A. Powell. 147: t.l. Nicholas Conte/bruce Coleman, Inc.; b.l. H. Armstrong Roberts; r. Bob Daemmrich/Stock Boston. 152: Michael McDermott for MMSD. 153: t. Colorado Historical Society. 155: l. Phil Schofield/AllStock; b.r. Monty Rossel. 156: t.l. The Granger Collection. 162: Mark E. Gibson. 163: Myron Wood/Photo Researchers. 164: John Ulven/Plimoth Plantation. 166: Candace Cochrane/Positive Images. 168: l. Baltimore Historical Society. 169-170: The Granger Collection. 171: The Bettmann Archive. 172: t. Archive/Levick; l. Rafael Macia/Photo Researchers, Inc. 173: m. Francis Westfield for MMSD. 178: b.l. The Granger Collection; l. Uniphoto Picture Agency. 181: Monica Stevenson for MMSD. Unit 6 182: b.r. The Bettmann Archieves; r. Thompson/The Stock Market. 186: The Bettmann Archives. 187: t. Andre Jenny/Unicorn Stock Photos; b. Peter Gridley/FPG International. 190-191: Stan Ries. 191: t. John M. Roberts/Stock Boston. 192: b. Fotografia Prod.J. Houck/Westlight; t. Stuart L. Craig, Jr/Bruce Coleman. 193: b.r. Aneal Vohra/Unicorn Stock Photos; b.l. Flip Schulke. 194: Monica Stevenson for MMSD. 195: Superstock. 196: l. Monica Stevenson for MMSD; l. Superstock; r. Monica Stevenson for MMSD; r. Jeffrey W. Myers/Stock Boston. 197: l., t. Monica Stevenson for MMSD; b. Susan Lampton for MMSD; t. Mug Shots/ The Stock Marekt. 198-199: Monica Stevenson for MMSD. 200-201: Monica Stevenson for MMSD. 200: l., r. courtesy of Project Bridge/Houston. 201: r. Monica Stevenson for MMSD. l. courtesy of Project Bridge/Houston. 202: l. Gamma-Liaison; r. Superstock. 203: l. James P. Blair/National Geographic Society; r. Odyssey/Frerck/Chicago. 204: Uniphoto, Inc. 204-205: Monica Stevenson for MMSD. 205: t. Norman Owen Tomalin/Bruce Coleman; b. Monica Stevenson for MMSD. 206: b. Jeff Vanuga/Westlight; t. Monica Stevenson for MMSD. 206-207: Monica Stevenson for MMSD. 207: Anne Nielsen for MMSD. 213: Monica Stevenson for MMSD. Endpapers: Bridgeman Art Library.

(continued from page ii)

Acknowledgments

The World Is Big, The World Is Small words and music by Ella Jenkins © 1966 by River Bend Music, Inc. Copyright assigned to Ella Jenkins © 1968. Published by Ell-Bern Publishing Co. Used by permission of Ell-Bern Publishing Co.

"Money's Funny" from Nuts to You and Nuts to Me by Mary Ann Hoberman. Copyright © 1974 by Mary Ann Hoberman. Gina Maccoby Literaryt Agency.

"What Was It Like" from Snippets by Charlotte Zolotow. Copyright © 1993 by Charlotte Zolotow. HarperCollins Publishers.

The book cover of **One Afternoon** by Yumi Heo, Copyright © 1994, published by Orchard Books, is reprinted by permission of the publisher.

The book cover of **Mike Mulligan and His Steam Shovel** by Virginia Lee Burton, Copyright © 1938, published by Houghton Mifflin, is reprinted by permission of the publisher.

The book cover of **My Map Book** by Sara Fanelli, Copyright © 1995, published by HarperCollins, is reprinted by permission of the publisher.

The book cover of **Together** by George Ella Lyon, Copyright © 1989, published by Orchard Books, is reprinted by permission of the publisher.

The book cover of **Anansi The Spider** by Gerald McDermott, Copyright © 1986, published by Henry Holt and Company, is reprinted by permission of the publisher.

The book cover of **One Hundred Is a Family** by Pat Munoz Ryan, Copyright © 1994, published by Hyperion Books, is reprinted by permission of the publisher.

The book cover of **Road Builders** by B. G. Hennessy, Copyright © 1994, published by Viking, is reprinted by permission of the publisher.

The book cover of **Melis Diner** by Marissa Moss, Copyright © 1992, published by Birchwater Books, is reprinted by permission of the publisher.

The book cover of **Work Song** by Gary Paulsen, Copyright © 1997, published by Harcourt Brace & Company, is reprinted by permission of the publisher.

The book cover of **The Great Monarch Butterfly Chase** by R. W. N. Prior, Copyright © 1993, published by Bradbury Press, is reprinted by permission of the publisher.

The book cover of **Around the Pond: Who's Been** Here by Lindsay Barret George, Copyright © 1996, published by Greenwillow Books, is reprinted by permission of the publisher.

The book cover of **World Water Watch** by Michelle Koch, Copyright © 1993, published by Greenwillow Books, is reprinted by permission of the publisher.

The book cover of **Treasure Nap** by Juanita Havill, Copyright © 1992, published by Houghton Mifflin Co., is reprinted by permission of the publisher.

The book cover of **The Goat in the Rug** by Charles L. Blood, Copyright © 1976, published by Alladin Books, is reprinted by permission of the publisher.

The book cover of **Tell Me a Story, Mama** by Angela Johnson, Copyright © 1989, published by Orchard Books, is reprinted by permission of the publisher.

The book cover of **Happy Birthday, Martin Luther King** by Jean Marzollo, Copyright © 1993, published by Scholastic, is reprinted by permission of the publisher.

The book cover of **Honest Abe** by Edith Kunhardt, Copyright © 1993, published by Greenwillow Books, is reprinted by permission of the publisher.

The book cover of **Weddings** by Ann Morris, Copyright © 1995, published by Lothrop, Lee & Shepard Books, is reprinted by permission of the publisher.

The Princeton Review
—— Handbook of ——
Test-Taking Strategies

S
T
A
N
D
A
R
D
I
Z
E
D

T
E
S
T

S
U
P
P
O
R
T

FILLING IN BUBBLES

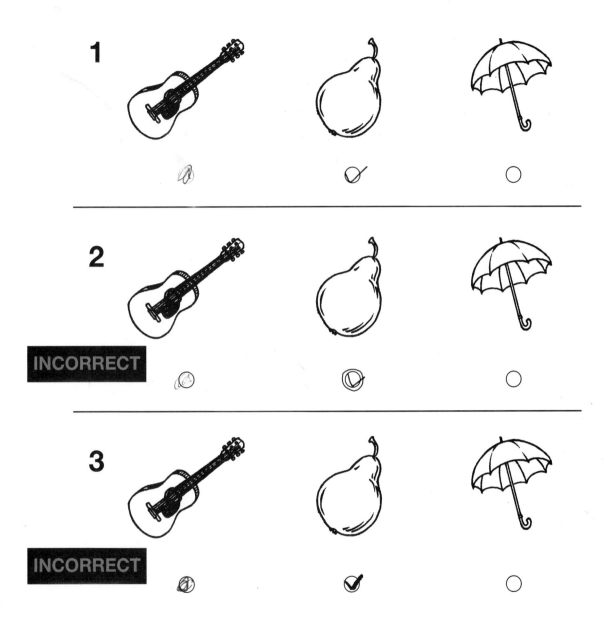

1

2 INCORRECT

3 INCORRECT

FILLING IN BUBBLES

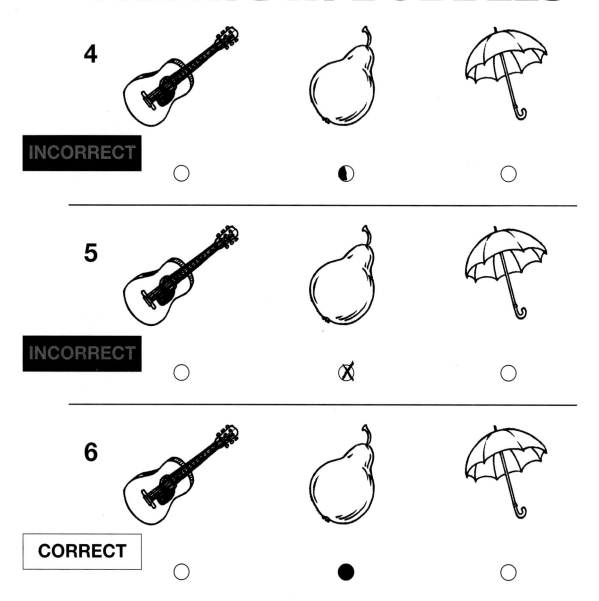

4 INCORRECT

5 INCORRECT

6 CORRECT

Remember: Do not write in your textbook.

LISTEN CAREFULLY

1    ○   ○   ○

2      ○   ○   ○

LISTEN CAREFULLY

3

○　　　　　○　　　　　○

4

○　　　　　○　　　　　○

Remember: Do not write in your textbook.

LISTEN CAREFULLY

1

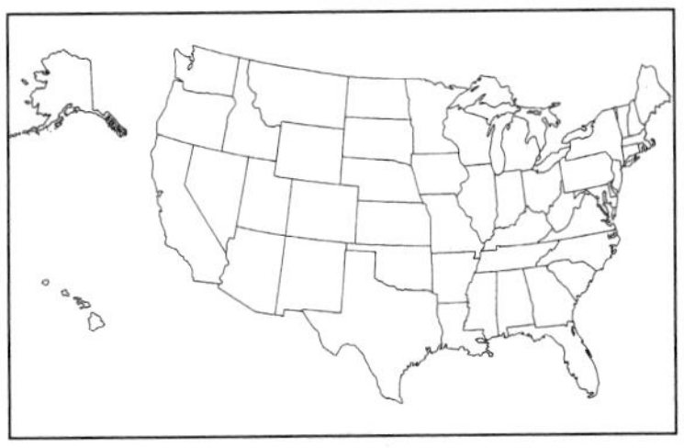

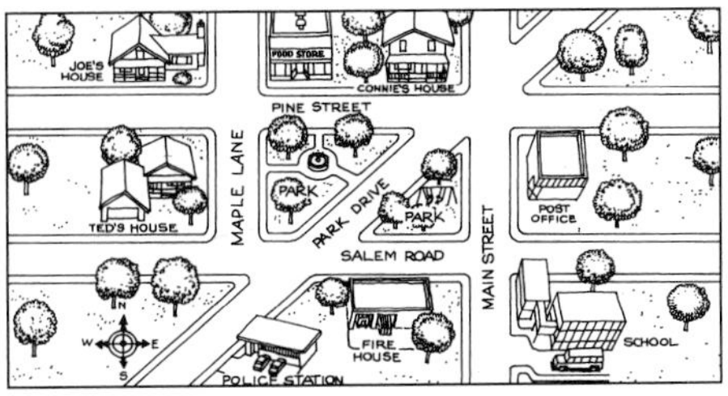

○   ○   ○

2

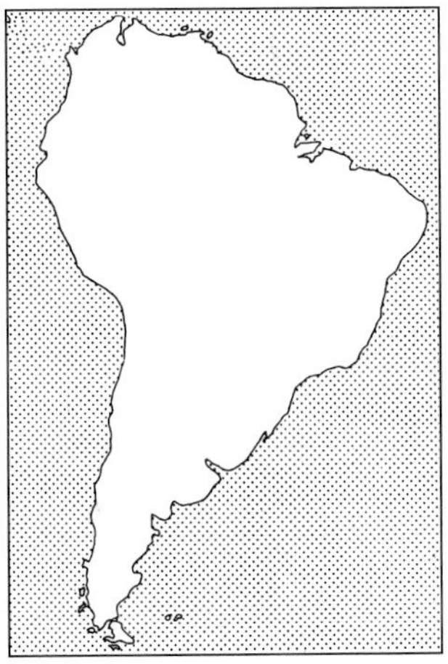

○   ○   ○

LISTEN CAREFULLY

3

○ ○ ○

4

○ ○ ○

Remember: Do not write in your textbook.

NUMBERED ANSWERS

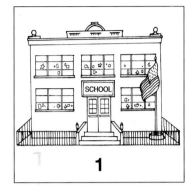

1

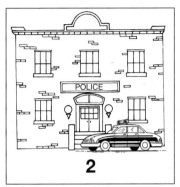

2

3

4

1

1	2	3	4
○	○	○	○

2

1	2	3	4
○	○	○	○

Remember: Do not write in your textbook.

NUMBERED ANSWERS

 **1**
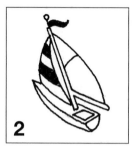 **2**
 **3**
 **4**

1

1 ○   2 ○   3 ○   4 ○

2

1 ○   2 ○   3 ○   4 ○

Remember: Do not write in your textbook.

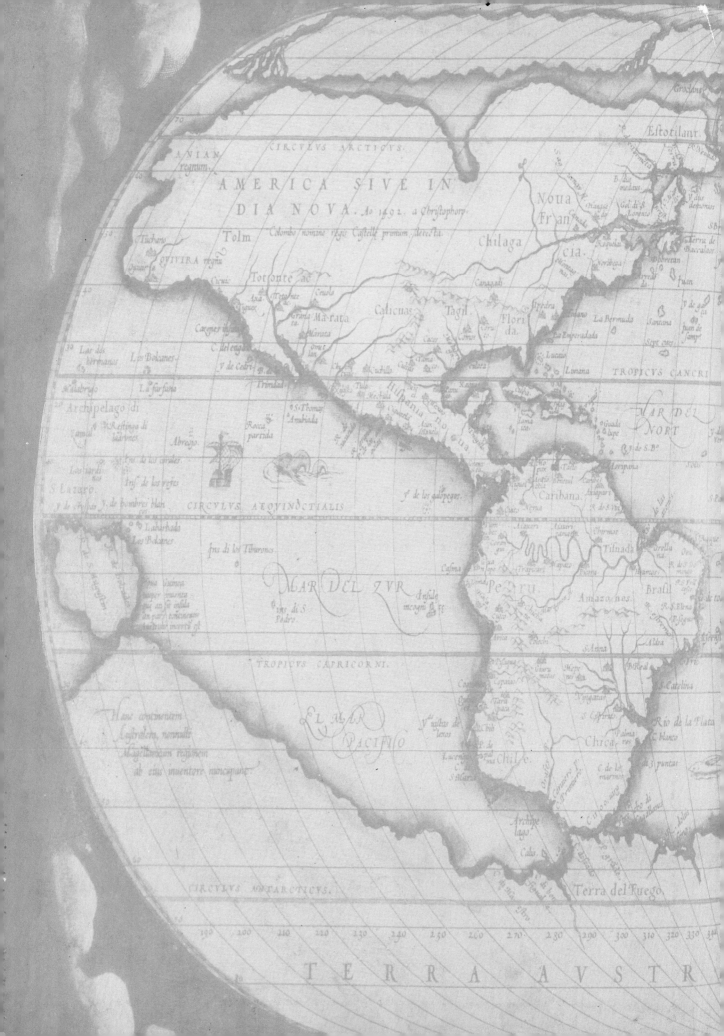